My Travels Through Southern Spain Nerja And The Surrounding Areas

by

Peter Thurgood

My love affair with Nerja and this particular area of Andalucia in Spain stemmed originally from my business, which involved selling and renting properties there. I had to visit the area quite a lot, and the more I did, the more I came to love it.

I have tried to convey here, the feelings that I got when I first visited Nerja and the surrounding areas. The feelings of freedom, of a strong nation, with a sense of history and pride. Maybe also a feeling of nostalgia on my part; nostalgia for a Britain long gone

What I found in this part of Spain was something that I felt my country had lost long ago. I have described here, the delights of simply being able to drive your car along a coastal road, and to be able to pull over onto a beach, when and where you want to. To be able to sit in a bar or restaurant for as long as you want to, without being turfed out by a greedy owner, who just wants to take more money. To get delicious free tapas with every drink and to look forward to what your next course will be.

I have also done my best to describe the Spanish customs and food and drink. In fact food and drink play a very large role in my life, especially when I am in Spain. After all, we cannot live without either can we?

I love Spanish people and their way of life, and have found during my travels in this area that one of the best ways to meet the people and get to know them is to eat and drink with them.

This book is dedicated to the pleasure seekers and freedom lovers of this world, please enjoy it.

Chapter 1

'We got this wine especially for you, it's a Rioja, would you like me to pour you a glass?' 'Have you ever known me to say no?' I answered, after all, I wasn't driving, and the food had been excellent. My wife and I were at a friend's house in London for dinner, it was a particularly cold February night, and as often happens on such occasions, the conversation gradually got around to summer holidays and warmer climes, where everyone had been, where they were going this year, and why they loved certain places more than others. Our hosts knew of course, that at that time, my business was dealing with holiday rentals in Nerja and other nearby towns and villages, and that I travelled there quite a lot, but the other couple present, did not, so when they asked me where my favourite destination was, I obviously came up with Nerja.

It's not that I haven't been anywhere else in the world, because I have, in fact I have travelled to something like 80 different destinations over the years, but the honest truth is that I just love Nerja so much, I wouldn't spend so much time there if I didn't. 'But why do you spend so much time there, don't you get fed up with it?' the woman next to me asked, 'we went there once some years ago, but quite frankly, I prefer Majorca, there's so much more for tourists to do there'.

So much more for tourists to do there? The way some people speak, you would think tourists were all mindless herds, grouped together in large groups, and being led into the Hotel Don Burro, by someone holding aloft a yellow clipboard, 'please try to keep together, and take your seats as quickly as possible, the show starts in 10 minutes, and we must be out of here by 3 pm to make way for the next group, now if anyone prefers tea instead of sangria please let me know by raising your hands now?'

Maybe that is the key to what makes Nerja appeal to me so much. It is not like Majorca or Benidorm or Torremolinos, where there are huge hotel blocks standing shoulder to shoulder, offering bingo and floor shows for the tourists. Nerja is still a part of real Spain, a place which certainly caters for the tourist, but also offers a chance for them to think for themselves and to live the real Spanish life if they want to, if only for a couple of short weeks a year. It is very difficult to explain in just a few brief sentences over a dinner table, what makes Nerja and that particular stretch of the coast so special, apart from the lack of bingo that is, I think I ended up saying something like I have to go there so much because of my work, but when I got home that night I felt angry with myself for not elaborating more. Of course I do go there because of my work, but I can assure you that is not the only reason I go there, I go there because I genuinely love it, and because it is a special place, which I have not found the equivalent of anywhere else in all the 80 something places throughout the world that I have visited over the years.

I decided there and then to put my thoughts down in writing, to explain to people why Nerja is something special, and not just another holiday resort. When I actually started to write this book however, I suddenly realised that there is no immediate solution that I could put down upon the first page, no single phrase that could possible sum up how I felt. There are hundreds, possibly thousands, of reasons why I love Nerja, and what makes it such a special place, so what I decided to do, was to put as many of these down as I can think of, so that you can sum them up for yourself, and hopefully taste a few samples of what makes Nerja such a wonderful and special place.

In order to truly enjoy Nerja, you should firstly try to understand something of not just Nerja, but Spain itself, its history, and most importantly, its people and their characteristics. Spain is a very large country, covering some 504,784 sq km, with a population of 39.7 million people. The natural enthusiasm for life of the Spanish people and the wonderful, almost round the clock sunshine, has been drawing visitors from all over Europe's more cold and damp countries for decades, but Spain is so much more than the Costas, beaches, and sunburnt tourists. It is a country drenched in the historical pageantry of empire and conquistadors, the artistic legacy of Goya, Velázquez, Picasso and Dalí, and the romance of Don Quijote, Ernest Hemingway and the International Brigade. But, religion of course, has also played a major role in shaping the Spain that we know today.

Spain, is a nation state born out of religious struggle between Catholicism and, in turn, Islam, Judaism, and Protestantism. After centuries of the Reconquista, in which Christian Spaniards fought to drive out the Moors, the Spanish Inquisition sought to complete the religious purification of the Iberian Peninsula by driving out the Jews, the Protestants, and other non-believers. The Inquisition was finally abolished only in the 1830s, and even after that, religious freedom was denied in practice, if not in theory. Catholicism became the state religion in 1851, when the Spanish government signed a Concordat with the central government of the Roman Catholic Church that committed Madrid to pay the salaries of the clergy and to subsidise other expenses of the Roman Catholic Church. This pact was renounced in 1931, when the secular constitution of the Second Spanish Republic imposed a series of anticlerical measures that threatened the church's very existence in Spain and provoked its support for the Francisco Franco uprising five years later.

The Spain which most tourists see today looks easy going and laid back, but that has not always been the way. Spain has had to carve out their relatively new way of life, from a very hard style of existence fraught with wars and religious persecution, with most people just managing to scrape out a living, either on the land, or from the sea. Tourism of course, has brought a new found wealth to much of Spain, especially the coastal regions, and as even more tourists converge on Spain, so a great many of them have also started to discover the joys and pleasures of other areas besides the costas, and consequently, more and more visitors have returned, not just for yet another holiday, but to take up residence in this wonderful country. So where we could once describe a typical Spanish town and its inhabitants, as having this or that characteristic, and speaking in this or that dialect, we now have a truly intermingled blend of races, characteristics, and dialects, which of course has happened very much so in Nerja, and has helped shape it to become the truly wonderful town it is today.

Nerja's foundation date is unknown, but it seems that it existed as a town in the times of Aberramán III. The first written information about Nerja is by the Arabic poet Ibn Sadí, a traveller who passed through in the year 917 and who referred to it as a hamlet, but nearly as big as a town, surrounded by leafy markets, and admired by all that lived there or passed through. The Arabs gave it the name, Naricha or Narija (abundant spring). It was formed in part during Muslim reign of Rayya and the local population settled under the protection of the ruler's castle, whose remains can still be seen today in the angle that forms the road to Frigiliana and the crossroad with the local quarry. Before this date there is no reference of settlements in the area that Nerja occupies, nevertheless, certain theories assume a form of human habitat during the Upper Palaeolithic age, which dates back to between 10,000 to 40,000 years ago, and evidence was found to support this in the now famous Nerja Caves. There is also evidence near to the centre of Nerja, where a Roman settlement existed, a hypothesis derived from the closeness of the Roman town of Detunda (Maro).

In June 1500, after the Duke of Nájera conquered Vélez, Nerja was by this time already Christian. The Muslim population there however were granted permission to remain with all their properties. After the Mudéjar uprising, and consequential leaving of the area, Doña Juana granted resettlement for the old Christians, who then occupied the abandoned dwellings, and she decreed that they should be free of paying taxes and of all other services, petty theft or impositions, privileges that were confirmed by Philip III and Philip IV.

At the end of the 18th Century, Nerja had a town council formed with two mayors, three M.P.s and an elected representative starting the municipal independence at the start of the 19th Century.

In 1509, the castle on the cliffs was rebuilt and only then did Nerja as we know it, begin to take shape. The local population, by then made up of relocated Spaniards from the north of Spain, began to build houses and other buildings around the fortress and along the coast. A full defensive system comprising castles and watchtowers spanned the coastline at this time and protected the coast by lighting fires which in turn warned the next watchtower along of the impending danger. These towers remained, guarding Nerja until both castles were destroyed by the English in 1812 to prevent them from falling into the hands of the invading Napoleonic army. Later that century, Nerja was to witness two local disasters; one, the phylloxera plague that destroyed the vines and the second, a powerful earthquake that affected much of Málaga and Granada provinces. It wasn't until the arrival of the tourist boom in early 1960's that Nerja once again started to prosper.

Chapter 2

Nerja lies at the far eastern reaches of the Costa Del Sol. Not so long ago a tiny fishing village, Nerja is now a bustling cosmopolitan town combining Andalucían history with marvellous and dramatic scenery, and welcoming visitors in their thousands from all over the world. The Balcon de Europa, in the centre of Nerja, is probably the most visited area in the town, where it is not improbable to hear Italian, French, German, Scandinavian, English, and of course Spanish, spoken while taking in a ten minute stroll to take in the sites there. The Balcon was once a fortress but today forms a fantastic centrepiece to the town and is loved by visitors and locals alike. High arches form wonderful viewpoints to the cliffs and beaches below while horses take shelter, along with their carriages, in the shade, awaiting passengers for their trips around the town. Ancient canons still stand guard pointing out to a sea which once spurned pirates and invaders; today they simply add a touch of history to many a photograph.

When one looks at Nerja today it is difficult to believe that as recently as the 1950s its main industry was fishing, and that the bars, restaurants and shops, were then small houses, inhabited by mainly poor fishermen and their families. Today it still relies a lot on the fishing industry, mainly to serve to the tourists, who now eat the majority of the fish. It will never become a sprawling giant like Benidorm or Torremolinos, with their line upon line of huge skyscraper hotels, because the local authorities have been careful to ensure that building regulations are strictly adhered to, limiting the height of all new buildings. Many new developments have been built to cater to the ever growing number of tourists and new residents, but unlike other areas of the Costa del Sol where tower blocks reign supreme, most of Nerja's new building projects are built to resemble Andalucían villages and combine traditional concepts with up to date leisure facilities.

In the town centre, a maze of blindingly white houses line the narrow streets as they wind their way to the cliff tops, with major Blue Flag beaches at each end of the town. In between the houses you will find plenty of shops, bars, cafés and restaurants to cater to the eclectic mix of people who seem to be forever window shopping, or eating or drinking. Many of the shops cater simply to the tourist trade but more and more are seeing the benefits of year round resident trade. Restaurants serve up French escargot, Greek souvlaki, Italian pizza, Mexican fajitas, English fish and chips, or is it Spanish fish and chips? Not forgetting of course, the many Spanish restaurants and tapas bars serving up local specialities, probably the most famous being, paella. In fact, take a trip down to Burriana beach and you will see the paella in all its glory, cooked in huge pans on red-hot wood burning fires. Nerja is still, first and foremost, a Spanish town, inhabited mostly by Spanish people, who just happen to cater for tourists, mainly the British.

Of all the paellas cooked in the huge pans on Burriana Beach, none can beat those cooked at Ayo's, which is a huge sprawling, open air chiringuito, at the far eastern end of the beach, open seven days a week, and continually packed with holiday makers and locals alike. Ayo is the owner, who also cooks the paellas, and what a character he is, dressed in shirt and shorts, with something on his legs that look like a cross between leg warmers and cricket pads, but in reality, are a sort of home made guard against the intense heat of the huge fires on which he cooks his paellas.

It was in fact Ayo, who on January 12th, 1959, when he was just a boy, discovered quite by chance, the now famous caves of Nerja. He was out playing with five of his friends in the hills near Maro when he saw a bat fly out of an opening in the ground. Like most young boys, he and his friends were adventurous to say the least, and so they started to dig around the hole, to widen it, in the hope that they would find more bats inside. What they found when the hole was big enough for them to shine a torch down there, was an enormous cavern, so big that they couldn't even see to the bottom.

The boys kept the cave a secret for a while, feeling that it was their cave. They went there every day and excavated more, gradually finding more openings, which they could actually climb down into. There were bats down there all right, but there were also other things, like strange markings on the walls and pieces of bone here and there. By this time the boys knew that what they had discovered was much more than just a bat cave, and it was now time to tell someone else, even though it would mean having to share their secret place with the grown ups of the town. What they never envisaged was that it wouldn't be just their parents and relations that would show an interest in their find, the whole of Spain became interested, and eventually the caves of Nerja, as they became known, became world famous, and put Nerja, as we now know it, on the map, and started the tourist boom there.

Legend has it, that the local government felt so indebted to the boys, that they offered to put them all through college and set them up in business in whatever professions they decided to choose, two became lawyers, another two, doctors, another a banker, but all Ayo wanted, was to own his own restaurant on the beach. It didn't seem much to ask, when put into perspective with the other boy's ambitions, but Ayo is doing very well indeed from his chosen profession, and I doubt very much if any of his friends are earning as much as he is today.

When you visit Ayo's, do have a chat with him, his English is not perfect, but then maybe you might decide to practise your bit of Spanish on him, he is always pleased to have a little chat with customers, especially those who ask about his discovery of the caves. He will even show you some old black and white photos taken at the time, showing him and his friends with local dignitaries, including among others, the Generalissimo himself, General Franco.

Ayo is a great character, recognised wherever he goes in the town, and always being filmed, sometimes just by tourists, other times by foreign film crews. He is also involved in local politics, although I am not sure in what respect. I did see him once, when the new Plaza de los Congrejos opened near Torrecilla Beach, and they held a big open air party there, where Ayo, as one would expect, cooked the Paella.

Burriana Beach is over one kilometre in length, making it the longest beach in Nerja. Apart from Ayo's, which is at the far eastern end, it also has numerous other chiringuitos, which are beach restaurants, serving food and snacks all day and well into the evening. There are also coffee bars, open-air drinks and ice cream stalls, news stands, cyber-cafés and shops selling all the usual tourist paraphernalia. The beach itself is very wide and consists of fine sand and gentle slopes to the sea, making it safe for people and children of nearly all ages. There are of course the usual sun beds and umbrellas to be hired, as well as various different water sports, such as canoeing, paragliding, diving, etc or just sailing.

In the height of summer, parking can be quite difficult there, but when and if you do manage to find a space, it is relatively cheap, to what we have to pay in the UK. A day's parking costs you just under one Euro. In London, you would be hard pressed to find a parking space for ten minutes for this price. If you do not wish to drive, there is a regular bus service that links Burriana beach with the centre of town, or alternatively you can also reach it walking, which takes approximately 10 minutes, but be warned, when walking back, it is uphill all the way, and after one of Ayo's paellas, and a bottle of wine, it could take you as long as twenty five minutes to half an hour.

Many of the bars and chiringuitos along Burriana, put on entertainment during the evening, quite often Flamenco shows, but during the day, the entertainment is performed by what we would probably call buskers, or street entertainers, although at the time of writing, it seems that the local police are trying to phase them out for some reason.. One of my favourites entertainers is a man that plays the accordion. There are quite a few accordion players now along this stretch of the coast, many of them hailing from eastern Europe, they usually play two or three tunes, accompanied, sometimes very badly, by another man on a tambourine, who then comes round to collect contributions from the diners. This doesn't sound too bad, but it can be pretty disconcerting, when they are almost lining up, one after the other, to play their few tunes to you and collect your ever dwindling piles of loose change.

But, my favourite, whom I call Mister Accordionista, not only plays for something like twenty to thirty minutes, but he is also an excellent musician, and will play requests if you ask him, and all for the same little scrap of loose change that you would pay the bad players for their lousy two numbers.

I accept that not everyone wants to listen to musicians while they are eating or drinking, but I personally believe that as long as they are not too intrusive, and do not stand too close to tables or actually ask for money, then to me there is nothing wrong with this, in fact I do quite like it, I think it adds to the atmosphere. I was in a restaurant in Nerja once, when a rather poor looking man came to the doorway, not inside, just at the doorway, and started playing his accordion. He wasn't marvellous, but he wasn't too bad either, he did about four or five numbers and then came around the tables with a small cardboard box, collecting whatever he could. Two English women who were sitting quite close to me, waved him away from them as though he were some bad smell. He just smiled and went onto the next table, and eventually left, waving to everyone and saying thank you to all. One of the English women stated in a very loud voice that people like him should be arrested. I couldn't believe my ears, if she didn't like his music, or didn't like his intrusion, that was fair enough, but to say he should have been arrested, this wasn't justified as far as I was concerned. In the UK we have street beggars who sit in doorways, and offer nothing at all apart from asking for spare change. At least street musicians are offering us something.

But even as I write this, Spain is changing its laws regarding street musicians, banning live music, and even confiscating guitars, can you imagine this, in the land of the guitar? But one of the biggest problems seems to be that there are three different levels of police, all with a different set of rules, never consistently enforced. The Guardia Civil seem to like musicians and don't see it as their job to hassle them, or to inform them that they could be arrested. It is the local police, the Guardia Urbana who are expected to enforce the music ban, but there seems to be an exception to this rule as well, depending in which town this "terrible" offence is taking place.

Malaga, for instance, seems to be turning a blind eye to it at the moment, as I found out when I was there just a few weeks ago. I was sitting at an open-air cafe next door to the Cathedral, which is a really beautiful setting. First to appear were two "musicians", one of whom played the trumpet, accompanied by his partner on the usual tambourine. They were appalling, loud and intrusive, and in my opinion, about as musical as a pair of cats having a fight on a tin roof. Luckily for me, they only played three numbers and then left, but already waiting in the wings, were two more. This time, the lead played a very loud clarinet, and his accompanist played an instrument which he unfolded like a collapsible trampoline, the likes of which I have never seen before, but which was based somewhere upon the lines of a home made xylophone, but with wires, which he proceeded to whack as hard as he could with two little hammers. This pair made the first pair look like concert musicians. Three tunes later they had finished. I looked around and thanked God that at last I could relax, as there didn't seem to be anyone else waiting to step onto the street stage. Then out of the corner of my eye, I saw a small fattish lady, in a bright flowery dress and a flower in her hair, eying us up. At least she didn't have an instrument, so maybe she was just a local crank, I thought. She then approached our table, and started to talk to my wife. I immediately turn my head away when this sort of thing happens, making out that I haven't even heard the person. I could hear her asking my wife if she was French, or Italian, Spanish maybe, English? My wife foolishly said yes at this point, and the lady started to sing right into her face. I couldn't recognise a tune, just an awful caterwauling noise. I span round to face her and just said 'Oh no, please?' To which the woman stopped immediately, said sorry and quickly left. I felt a little sorry for her as I am not usually rude to anyone, but the words had just come out before I could stop them. After that, peace returned to the area and we were able to continue our meal in without further interruption.

I have heard that in Valencia, they just chase off all 'non-traditional Spanish' street performers, where that would have left our trio, I don't know! From what I have heard, a lot depends on how the local police feel at the time, and if they particularly like the music that is being played. If they do, it seems that they are willing to turn a blind eye for an hour or three. Whatever the outcome of all this will be, you can bet your life that EU rules and regulations are the ulterior motif behind it.

Musicians, however, are not the only people that one has to contend with, and Nerja, like almost every town or city in the world now, has its fair share of street blaggers of one type or another, from straight forward beggars, to people working some sort scam or another. There is a man, quite well dressed, who travels the streets of Nerja, stopping at restaurants and bars. He leaves a small piece of paper on each table, proclaiming that he is deaf and dumb, and that he is collecting to help others, so inflicted. As soon as he has laid out all his notes on the various table, he goes directly to the first table and starts picking them up again, with any donations that customers have left.

When I first encountered this particular person, I immediately assumed that he was working some sort of scam, as he shows no badge or anything official, not what I could see anyway. I also didn't know at the time that he was dumb, so I just thought what a cheek he had, going round to tables, not even bothering to speak to people and just begging for money.

It wasn't until one day when I was having a drink with a friend on mine that lives in Nerja, that this man came along again and shook hands with my friend. They communicated through sign language and the man left. After he had gone, my friend told me all about him. He told me that his name is Manolo, and that he came from a large family, who lived locally and were all born deaf and dumb, and that he started doing this when he was quite young in order to help support his family. From there, he formed a proper registered charity, and the rest is history. When I found all this out I felt really bad about the awful way I had thought about him, and ever since then have always tried to give him some change whenever I see him, and have become quite friendly with him. He never passes me without a friendly pat on the shoulder and a big smile, with or without my small change offerings. Manolo is a very nice man who deserves all the support he can get.

One of the funniest sights I ever saw in Nerja, was one day, whilst sitting in Ayo's on Burriana Beach, and watching the world go by, I noticed a speed boat pulling a very competent water skier, who was doing all types of fancy tricks, including jumps and backward turns where he would hold on with just one hand, while skiing backwards, all very impressive to say the least. Finally, as the boat came nearer to the shore, the skier let go, and glided perfectly up onto the beach. He then picked up his skis and walked over to a pile of clothes that he quickly changed into.

Now you must bear in mind that all the time I was watching him, it was from a distance, so I couldn't get a very clear view of what he actually looked like. I don't know what he actually did with his skis, but by now he was completely dressed and swaggering towards Ayo's with a large package under one arm. When he finally got there, I could see that he was now wearing an ill fitting jacket and trousers, with a vest underneath, and a little trilby hat on his head. He was about five feet tall, and a very scraggy looking sixty to seventy years old. The package under his arm turned out to be two pictures in frames, which he then took around the tables, trying to sell. The first picture was of a cat and the other, a picture of Jesus. As he stopped at each table, he slightly moved the pictures up and down, which caused an effect, which made the pictures look as if the eyes were opening and closing as the pictures were moved. I had never seen anything so repulsive in my life, and who on earth, I asked myself, would go to a beachside restaurant, and end up buying such awful rubbish? What really struck me as funny, however, was the fact that from a distance, this man had looked like the perfect all action hero, I would imagine that there were many women there that day who couldn't take their eyes off him whilst he was performing his water act, but to see this little old man afterwards, trying to sell these ghastly pictures, was something else. But you had to give him seven out of ten for trying, and definitely ten out of ten for his water skiing.

Burriana Beach is a great place for people watching, its wide promenade that runs almost the full length of the beach, divides the chiringuitos and restaurants from the actual beach itself. At the western end of the beach you can still see the fishing boats and the fishermen repairing their nets, whilst directly above them, perched high on a cliff top, is the Parador, one of Spain's national run hotels. There is a lift from beach level that takes you right up to the Parador. Also from this spot, a roped off walkway starts, which takes you along, through craggy rock faces and little coves, finally coming out near to the start of Calle Carebeo, which is one of the main streets of Nerja. The walkway used to lead right to the Balcon de Europa, but for some reason unbeknown to me, they closed off that last section some years ago.

Walking in an eastwardly direction along Burriana Beach, takes you past all the chiringuitos, bars, shops, etc., and finally come to an end at an enormous cliff face that juts out into the sea. If you swam around this cliff face you would eventually come to Maro, which is the next little town just past Nerja.

Burriana Beach does not just house bars and restaurants, there is, of course, plenty of living accommodation there as well, mainly in the shape of six apartment blocks, which have been built recently, late 1990s to early 2000s. They are only four stories high and have large terraces overlooking the sea. Also, because of Nerja's geographical formation, much of it is built into the cliffs and hillsides, so if you stand anywhere on Burriana Beach with your back to the sea, and look upwards, you will see some absolutely beautiful villas sitting right on top of the cliffs in front of you. Also, cut right into the hillside, is a really lovely development called Capistrano Playa. This is a collection of houses and apartments, surrounded by tropical gardens, an ornamental lake and a waterfall. It is such a beautiful setting that newly weds, often have their wedding photos taken here.

But the beach itself is what most people go to Burriana for, especially families with children. It is wide, and most importantly, very safe, with its gentle slopes and pedestrianised walkway. You can watch people all day long, with their weird antics and sometimes even weirder clothes sense, but to watch children playing innocently and happily in the sand and the sea, is a joy in itself. When I worked as an agent for rental properties in Nerja, I often got asked by caring parents, what is there to do for children? Now I know these parents are doing what they think is best for their children, but sometimes I think they need to take one step back, and look again from a different perspective. You can give children the most expensive and sophisticated toys and games in the world, but at the end of the day, a straight forward bucket of muddy sand and another of water, and most children are more than happy. I once watched a bunch of kids playing on a pile of beach-bed mattresses on the beach, and they couldn't have been happier.

I also recently noticed a new game which quite a lot of local children seem to be playing, which involves, of all things, rubber flip-flops. The children, mostly boys, are each armed with a rubber flip-flop and a pack of some sort of swappable picture cards. The game seems to be played something along the lines of Boule or bowls, where one flip flop is thrown first, and the other have to throw their flip flops as close to it as possible, with the picture cards being the prizes for the winner. Don't ask me why these kids chose flip-flops with which to play this game, or where it originated from, because I do not know, but it has certainly spread along the coast, as I have seen children playing it in Almuñécar and Torre del Mar, as well as Nerja. So now you know what to do if your offspring tell you that they are bored and have nothing to play with, just take off one of their flip-flops and throw it, and tell them to stop moaning and get on with the game.

Another question I often used to get asked, usually regarding properties, is, is it child friendly? Now can anyone please tell me what does a child friendly house consists of? A child can fall off a chair, so should we take all chairs out of the house, they can cut themselves with a kitchen knife, so should we not have any of these either? How about electric plugs and sockets? I'm afraid the real answer really lies with the parents, what these kids need are child friendly parents, who will watch them and play with them, and teach them that certain things can be dangerous to them. Better get off my hobby horse now, and get back to the beach before it runs away with me.

Back on Burriana, I was watching a group of musicians one day, who looked and sounded very much like the famous Gypsy Kings. They were only buskers, but they were excellent, and certainly attracted a large crowd, but as I watched them, I suddenly noticed one small boy, who had his back to the group, and seemed to be talking to a nearby tree on the beach. This intrigued me, so I went a little closer to try to find out exactly who he was talking to, but there was definitely no one else there. The boy was still looking at the tree and saying 'hello, hello,' then I heard an answer in a high pitched Spanish accent, 'hola, hola.' I walked right around the tree, expecting to see maybe a little friend of the boy, who was hiding and playing a game with him, but I couldn't find anyone. The boy looked at me as if I were mad, and then said 'hello' again. At this point I felt that I just had to ask him who he was talking to, with which he just pointed to a branch above my head where a large green parrot was sitting. 'Hola' said the parrot once again. It seemed that the parrot was owned by one of the chiringuitos, who let it have its freedom from its cage whenever it wanted, and it obviously became a very big attraction, especially to children.

The Gypsy Kings type group played around Nerja for a number of years, attracting large crowds wherever they played. The only person that didn't seem very keen on them playing in his place was Ayo. I don't know why this was, as when they did play there, the majority of the customers seemed to like them very much. I watched one lunch time, when they had to sit outside in the blazing hot sun, and wait for nearly half an hour before Ayo finally allowed them to play under the shade of the grape vines that make up his roof. The last time I saw them, was one night when they came into a restaurant in town, called Refugios, where I was eating. They hadn't come in to play, just to have a drink at the bar, and to share out their day's takings, which didn't look very much to me from where I was sitting. I bought them a drink and asked them why I hadn't seen much of them lately. They spoke their own distinct version of Spanish, which I found very difficult to understand, but from the little I did pick up, along with the hand gestures, it seemed to me that they were being driven out of Nerja by someone or something which I did not quite understand. Maybe it was a dwindling interest in their type of music, as they were playing to mostly tourists, who on the whole, seem to prefer something a little more gentle on the ears, or maybe it was something to do with the local police, whom, I am told, can often be just a little bit unsympathetic, when dealing with Gitanos. Whatever the reason, I haven't seem them since, which I think is such a shame, as they were a good, friendly, and enthusiastic bunch of musicians.

Chapter 3

Nerja's main square takes in the Balcon de Europa and runs to the beautiful old church of El Salvador. This whole area is lined with palm trees and flower beds. There are restaurants and open air cafes, as well as two really pretty old fashioned ice cream stalls, where women in lace aprons serve every day, until 11pm. These woman have served ice cream on their stalls for over 40 years, and their families have made and supplied ice cream for even longer. I do not eat ice cream, but my wife, Frances, loves it, and finds it difficult to pass the stalls without stopping to buy one. They are the best, she tells me.

As evening approaches, various stalls set up their businesses around the edge of the Balcon and the church, from the inevitable portrait artists, to people doing hair braiding, and selling hand made jewellery. There is also another artist whom I find absolutely amazing to watch. He works, accompanied by heavy metal rock from his portable CD player. He wears a protective face mask and produces pictures by using car paint sprayed from aerosol cans, and then dabbed and scraped and padded with pieces of paper, to eventually form wonderful paintings of what looks like lunar landscapes. Really fascinating!

There is one form of street entertainer however, which I personally, cannot stand, and that is the guys, or women, who dress up, as some sort of a statue, with their faces usually sprayed silver, and then stands motionless for hours on end, moving now and then to 'frighten' some small child, who obviously thought they were just a real statue. I think they probably buy their silly costumes from a shop somewhere that specialises in them, and then just stand there in them for the rest of the night. The trouble is, these people have become more and more popular in Nerja, and I have seen people just sitting and watching them for ages, and giving them money. I cannot believe it, you can see sillier outfits on some of the people on the beach, and you don't have to pay for the privilege of watching them.

My favourite act takes place right in front of the church at night, and it involves two dancers who dance the Tango. They are young and good looking and dance magnificently. To watch them you would believe that they are two young lovers, but in actual fact they are brother and sister. When they are dancing, it seems like half the population of Nerja are out there watching and photographing them. It is only when the music stops and they start to go around the crowd to collect donations, that the crowd disperses so quickly that you would be excused for thinking there had been a bomb alert. I have often thought that if the police wanted to disperse an unruly crowd very quickly, all they would need to do is take out a collecting tin or hat. It seems to have the desired effect when our two magnificent dancers do it.

I haven't seen the Tango dancers performing very much lately. I don't know if they have been stopped by the local police as well, but if you do get the chance to see them, they are well worth it, and I personally think it is something of a special treat to see them. They also own a shop selling leather goods in Calle Pintada. Probably the last time I saw them perform, was one night as I walked through the square, I caught them just starting up, which I thought was marvellous, as I could then get a front line view of them, instead of being stuck at the back of a huge crowd and trying to peer over everyone else's shoulders. Five minutes into their act, there suddenly erupted, one of the loudest noises I have ever heard. I think for a moments, people actually thought it could have been a bomb. The dancers stopped and everyone looked around, wondering where this awful noise had come from. There right outside the church was this guy with a mackintosh thrown over one shoulder and a pork pie hat stuck on the back of his head. He had a portable CD player, which he had turned up to full volume, and out blasted Frank Sinatra, singing 'My Way,' This guy then preceded to mime, very badly to this song. I have nothing against Frank Sinatra, or that particular song, but this was wrong, one hundred percent wrong. This talentless creep had stopped two really talented people, because his music was just so loud that it made it completely impossible to even hear their music. They packed up their equipment, music, etc., and left, and so did I.

I don't know what it is about the Balcon de Europa, it is like a magical place that draws you to it. I find it almost impossible to walk home at night without taking another trip to the end of the Balcon to look at the stars and the moon's reflection on the sea below, and all those twinkling little lights that represent the coastline, as far as you can see. After the Balcon, you come back to the church, with its beautiful square, and its floor that shines in the moonlight almost as if it has been wax polished. If you want to see the Balcon and the church at their best, go around midnight, after most people have gone home, when it is deserted, apart from yourself and your thoughts.

There is another thing, which I always class as magical in Nerja, it is the sound of a man who travels the streets, usually early in the morning, with a bicycle, from which he sharpens knives and scissors. He plays a set of pipes, which have a really haunting, almost sad sound about them, which echoes through the streets. I have never heard this sound anywhere else, and it has become to me, a real part of Nerja.

The Church of El Salvador, was built in 1697 on the site of the old castle chapel. It was enlarged in 1770, it now houses a magnificent mural of the Incarnation on a Nerja beach by one of the great masters of new European painting, Francisco Hernández, and a bronze Christ, like the statue at the western entrance to the town, by sculptor Aurelio Teno.

The Balcón de Europa, was built on the spot occupied by the Guards' Tower in Moorish times and constituted the starting point for present-day Nerja. Built in 1487, it was formerly a IX Century Castle, and it was the castle's chapel that later developed into the Church. Today, the Balcon houses a panoramic restaurant and a wonderful view point, plus of course, the two ancient cannons which still form a reminder that until 1812 there was a fortress at the top of the cliffs.

Spanish people are in general, very proud of their culture and traditions, their celebrations and festivals, and have a wonderful way of preserving such culture. There are hundreds, if not thousands, of festivals held throughout Spain during the course of a year, with every town and village celebrating their own particular special days, and Nerja is no exception, with several taking place each year, each one a colourful, and usually noisy, extravaganza of costumes, music and festivities that often go on well into the night, and sometimes longer.

The first of the year, isn't actually a festival as such, it is the celebration of New Year's Eve, (Noche Vieja) which is a great time to be in Nerja. It is the highlight of the year. Everyone gathers on the Balcon de Europa at 11.30 pm in their best clothes; clutching a bottle of champagne or Cava, and a bunch of grapes. As the clock strikes midnight everyone eats their grapes, one for each stroke, which is a lot harder than you would imagine. On the strike of twelve the fireworks start and the band begins to play. It is a fantastic atmosphere, and one not to be missed. The town square is filled with revellers as local bands play and sing throughout the evening, and a huge fireworks display when the clock strikes twelve. According to tradition, all the women are supposed to wear red underwear for luck, but it has to be bought for them by someone else. Sounds to me that this is a tradition, which was made up by women, with women in mind.

Festival of the Three Kings (Fiesta de los Tres Reyes) is held on the night of 5th of January and is when the children can at last celebrate their 'Christmas Eve'. Children write their letters to Los Tres Reyes, telling them how good they have been throughout the year. If they have been badly behaved they are told they are likely to get no presents but a lump of coal (Carbon), instead. Carbon is on sale in the sweet shops, a kind of black sugar honeycomb, and is sometimes given to children as a joke if they have been naughty or mischievous during the year. A procession sets off from the Balcon de Europa at around 5pm., and makes its way through the surrounding streets, which are lined with people watching the floats passing by. The children dress up and the Three Kings throw sweets and confetti as they pass by. In the bakeries, Rosca de Reyes is on sale, this is a traditional ring shaped cake made out of sweet spicy dough and decorated with icing and dried fruits. Inside it contains small toys and charms, and it is considered lucky if you manage to find one of the charms.

The Fiesta de San Anton is the first real festival of the year. It takes place in Maro and involves a procession, and a display of fireworks, lasting two days from the 16th to the 17th January. Numerous bonfires are lit on the first day as an invocation for the protection of animals from illness. On the following day, a mass is celebrated and later there is a lively traditional verbena (fair - party with music).

The Nerja Carnival takes place over 3 days in February, with a large street parade, followed by the usual mix of music, dancing, and singing. The exact dates vary from year to year.

The Fiesta de Semana Santa (Holy Week) is predominantly, a procession held during holy week. March or April, each year, and is usually a very serious affair, where drinking etc, is very much frowned on by a large majority of the people. Every town and village in Spain has its own Fiesta and procession. Easter week processions compete with each other for splendour. Parades leave town churches to wend slowly through the streets carrying statues of Christ on the cross and the Virgin Mary in mourning. Religious brotherhoods (Hermandades) representing guilds of tradesman, in elaborate robes often with high pointed cowls covering their faces, carry the very heavy statues with a slow rocking gait accompanied by drum beat, incense and candles.

Cruces de Mayo, (May Crosses) held on the 3rd May has a long tradition in Nerja that has changed over time but has not been completely lost. What used to be an occasion for courtship among young people has become a popular fiesta based on the assembly of colourful floral altars that are placed on various streets and that give occasion for flamenco singing, dancing, eating and drinking. Around 30 crosses are set up, some of which are so popular that it is necessary to block off traffic from the streets where they are placed due to the crowds that flock to see them.

Noche de San Juan, takes place on the 23rd June and goes on through the night until 24th June. Barbecues are lit all over the beach, in a celebration of the burning of the "júas" (Judas dolls), the "moragas" (beach parties) and the ritual of submerging oneself in nine waves of the sea after leaping over the fire are performed on the beaches of Burriana, La Torrecilla and El Playazo, to wash away one's sins in the sea at midnight. During these celebrations free food is provided, and much drinking takes place.

Festival Cueva de Nerja is not a festival in the normal accepted sense of the word. It is a series of concerts, both flamenco and classical, which are held during July, in the Caves of Nerja.

Virgen del Carmen takes place on the evening of the 16th July. The much loved effigy of the Virgin is paraded through the streets, and then taken around the bay on a flower bedecked fishing boat, accompanied by a flotilla of "jábegas" (fishing boats). Brass bands play, and fireworks fill the late night sky. Needless to say, there is plenty of eating, drinking and singing.

Feria de las Maravillas takes place between 7th to the 9th of September, the 8th, being the local saint's day, the Virgen de las Maravillas. An image of the Virgin travels through the streets in a procession accompanied by a deafening "coheteá" (lighting of firecrackers). The costs are shared by residents depending on their economic status. This fiesta revolves around traditional music and beach parties that originated in the sixteenth century.

Feria de Nerja takes place between 8th to 12th October and is the local saint's day of Nerja. Playing host to a great fair and amusements, with lots of music and noise.
Christmas. Unlike the UK, Christmas decorations in public places do not start going up until December. Once started however, the celebrations become evident everywhere with Christmas markets and Christmas trees on sale on street corners. In recent years Nerja has become more commercial in it's outlook and now has Christmas music playing in shops and Carol services at various venues.

Christmas Eve, (Nochebuena) is very important and in households all over Spain special dishes will be created, including fish and seafood meals, which always feature high on the menu. Roast lamb is a popular dish, although turkey, I am sorry to say, is increasing in popularity. Turron (a kind of nougat) is traditionally served at Christmas as is Cava (sparkling wine).

After the main meal, the adults exchange gifts, but the children only get a small present at this time, having to wait until later for theirs. Father Christmas (Papa Noel) does not traditionally visit, as in other European countries, although traditions are changing, and some families are now adopting our traditions.

My favourite festival is the Romeria de San Isidro, which takes place on 15th May every year. The word Romeria derives from the Latin description of the ancient pilgrimage by foot to Rome. Whilst maybe not as far as Rome, the Nerja celebrations are also in the form of a pilgrimage, although somewhat shorter.

After attending a special mass at the Iglesia del Salvador at the Balcon de Europa the congregation, nearly all in traditional dress, head off on a colourful procession. Accompanied by people on horseback or in highly decorated carts drawn by bullocks. This is a very happy and noisy affair, with non-stop music, and of course, as is the Spanish way, plenty of food and drink to accompany them. They make their way from the church, on a special route through the town, and onto their final destination at the Caves of Nerja, near the village of Maro.

What then follows is an all day open-air party with even more music and dance as well as a non stop supply of locally produced wines and food. The partying continues well into the night and beyond, by which time the attendance regularly tops 5000 people. This is a festival that you must see if you are there in May, even if you don't make it as far as the caves, which is quite a walk, you will still have lots of fun, and I am sure, take lots of photos, from just watching it from its start in the town.

The festival is not solely for the Spanish inhabitants of Nerja either. I know one local English businessman, who lives there, who takes part in this festival every year, riding one of his favourite horses in the procession, alongside the Spanish riders, who believe me, take some beating, both for their horsemanship, and also especially for their elaborate costumes and the beautiful senoritas, who accompany them, riding side saddle behind them. But one of the funniest things I ever saw, was a write up about the festival, by an English woman, in a travel brochure, where she described the carts being pulled by the bullocks, 'where else' she wrote, 'can you see bullocks pulling colourful carts through the streets?' Doesn't sound or look funny? If you had seen her original text, where she had accidentally substituted the letter O instead of U in the word bullocks, I am sure you would have seen the joke.

This is a good example of how the misuse of just one letter in a word can completely alter the whole meaning of the word, and this is why I thoroughly recommend the visitor, or indeed the new resident, to try to learn as much as possible of the Spanish language. In much of Spain now, and Nerja is no exception, English is widely spoken, but you won't always find this, especially with the older generation, and also in parts of Nerja old town, where tourism still hasn't quite made its mark yet.

Believe me, you will enjoy yourself much more if you learn to converse with the locals in their own language, and in return they will accept you as someone who is interested in them and their language and culture, instead of just someone who is there for the sun and the cheap beer. We have all heard those stories about people who have sold up in the UK, bought a place in Spain, and have never spoken a word of Spanish since they arrived. And this is true, I have seen them and heard them, 'Oh they can understand us,' they say, 'anyway, we only mix with our own.'

No one has to speak another language, but try to think how you would feel if visitors from another country came to your country and point blankly refused to speak any English to you, that they just insisted that we must try to understand them instead?

We get visitors from some of the poorest and uneducated countries in the world come to Britain, yet still most of them can speak some English. If they can do it, so can you.

Here are just a few basic words and phrases that will help to get you started.

Hello" - "hola" *(OH lah)*
"Please" - "Por favor" *(POR fah-VOHR)*
"Thank you" - "Gracias" *(GRAH-see-ahss)*
"Can you help me?" - "Puede ayudarme?" *(PWEH-dhe ah-yoo-dh-AHR-meh)*
"I don't understand" -- "No comprende" - *(Noh kohm-PREHN-dho)*
"Where is...?" - "Donde esta...?" *(DHOHN-dheh ehs-TAH)*
"How far?" - "A que distancia?" *(Ah kay dhees-Tan-syah)*
"How much is it?" - "Cuanto cuesta?" *(KWAHN-toh KWEH-stah)*
"I don't like it" -- "No me gusta" - *(Meh GOOS-tah/No meh GOOS-tah)*
Asking for the check or bill at a restaurant: La cuente, por favor *(Lah KWEHN-tah)*

One word that is nearly always mispronounced by the British is the main word we are talking about here, which is 'Nerja'. So many people pronounce it with a 'hard' letter J, but in Spanish there is no hard J. The letter J is always pronounced soft, almost like the letter H, as in the man's name Juan, which should be pronounced as *'Hwun'*. But now comes the difficult bit, with the J being pronounced soft, you would be forgiven for thinking that Nerja should be pronounced *Nerha*, but it is not. It is pronounced locally as *"Nerka"*. Listen to the locals when they say it, you will soon pick it up.

And lastly, don't be embarrassed about rolling those Rs. When you are saying 'por favor' for instance, use the R at the end of 'por' as if it had a little motorbike attached to it, roll that tongue a little. Again, listen to the locals when they speak, I always find it is the best way of learning.

Chapter 4

Flamenco plays a major part in the culture of Spain, and Nerja is no exception to this. I have seen little girls, as young as four years old, dressed in traditional Flamenco dresses, being taught to dance and clap by their mothers. At the many festivals held in Nerja, you hear the traditional sounds of Flamenco guitarists and singers. You also hear modern music, much of it, very much influenced by the traditional sounds of Flamenco, but traditional or modern, you will still see the girls using the Flamenco style in the movements of their arms, as they dance.

There is a bar in the street, Plaza Cavana, which is next to the church, the bar uses the same name as the street, and was in fact, the first hotel in the town, but now exists solely as a bar. The bar was always used mostly by locals rather than tourists, with no direct outside seating, other than a shared part of the large terrace in the centre of the street, which several bars use. Since the smoking ban was introduced in Spain however, this bar, along with many others have had to introduce an outdoor seating area, or risk loosing a large part of their clientele. For many years it was usually the only bar in that street which was open late at night, after the tourist bars had closed, and it is here that I have heard some really good, impromptu Flamenco guitar being played, and this is not by buskers, playing for money, this is usually by dedicated musicians, who just want to play and appreciate the good participating audience that they get there, where everyone claps and some even take part in singing their part of whatever song is being played. I watched two elderly women in there one night, probably in their late sixties, who danced around each other, swishing their skirts, with arms raised above their heads, as everyone else clapped and 'oleyed' to the guitarist's music.

Nights like these are not a regular thing, and I relish every minute of them, this is real Spain.

There are, of course, several venues in Nerja, where you can hear and watch genuine Flamenco shows, but I must add, that as good as they are, they are mostly put on just for the tourists. There is however, one small bar, called Bar Tipico El Molino, which is in Calle San José, a small alleyway near the centre of town. The bar is located in an old oil mill in one of the oldest buildings still in use in Nerja today. There is no entrance fee here, and it has a great friendly atmosphere. If you do decide to pay El Molino a visit, try to ensure that you do not miss the midnight homage to the Salve Rociera 'El Ángelus,' sung for the Virgen del Rocío, the local saint, where all the lights are switched off, and the singers turn towards the saintly image, set in an alcove in the wall, and sing this song with great feeling.

Other singers and guitarists are encouraged to get up onto the small stage to perform, and many of them are excellent, although they will have their work cut out to beat Paco Gumersindo, who used to be the lead singer and guitarist there. Paco has such a powerful voice that no microphones are ever used or needed. One night when I was there, Paco had taken a break, and left the bar for a few minutes. Sitting close to me, and very near to the stage, was a large gentleman of obvious Gitano (Gypsy) extraction, accompanied by a young lad, which I think was his son. The Gitano suddenly got up and grabbed Paco's guitar, which he had left perched upon his vacant chair, and proceeded to play.

The Gitano was, as I had expected, very good, and as he played and sung in his very real, throaty, typical Gitano voice, so his son, who was still sitting near to me, started clapping in accompaniment to him. Within minutes he had the whole room clapping and shouting for more. After a couple of songs, Paco came back into the room, his eyes lit up with anger as he saw the Gitano playing his guitar, because not only was he playing the instrument that did not belong to him, without asking permission, he also had this trick where he would thump with the palm of his hand onto the wooden front of the guitar and follow up with a spin of the instrument. I could see that Paco was furious, this was an expensive guitar, and to have that enormous hand crashing down on it, time after time could obviously cause damage to it. Paco bounded up onto the stage and ripped it out of the Gitano's hands, stopping him in mid song. I don't know what he said to the man, as he did not shout, but spoke in a very low voice, up close to him. The audience was amazed, as most of them didn't know what was happening at all. But whatever it was that Paco had said, the huge man just quietly got to his feet, beckoned to his son and they left. I cannot guarantee that you will get a show like this every time in El Molino's, but I can guarantee that you will have a good time, and be thoroughly entertained, if Flamenco is what you are looking for.

Other people are encouraged to get up and sing or dance, in El Molino's, but it is generally accepted that they ask first, like one rather large lady, whom I used to see there quite often, she was very good, and would nearly always sing "Bésame Mucho," which is Mexican in origin, but has always been a particular favourite of mine. She might not have sung in strict Flamenco style, but she did sing with feeling, and that is what really matters. Around this same time, an Englishman, (I think), with sandy coloured hair and thick pebble glasses, used to frequent El Molino's quite a lot, and he would sit very quietly near the door with his wife, smiling and tapping his feet gently to the music. He would sit like this, without making a sound, until Paco started to sing "Guantanamera", (girl from Guantánamo), which is another South American song. The chorus of Guantanamera, goes, Guantanamera, guajira, Guantanamera, pronounced *(gwahn-tah-nah-MEH-rah, gwa-HEE-rah, gwahn-tah-nah-MEH-rah),* which roughly translates into English, as, "Guantanamera, dance (the guajira), Guantanamera". When Paco sang this song, he always invited the audience to join him in the chorus, and I have never seen anyone come to life as much as old Sandy did. He would jump to his feet and belt out, Guantanamera, guajira, Guantanamera, as loud as he could, so loud in fact that he even drowned Paco's singing. It was a really funny sight to see, as he would sit down in between each verse, and then jump up again when the chorus came back in, and he kept such a dead-pan face all the time. I think almost everyone in the place, including Paco, thought it was as funny as I did.

I say almost everyone, because there was one man, a Spaniard, although I didn't know he was at the time, who used to take his chair up onto the enormous concrete wheel, which was once part of the original olive press, and now forms a platform in front of the stage. The Spaniard, whom, because I didn't know his name, I called the Artist in Residence, would sit alone on the wheel, always dressed from head to foot in black, and always smoking a long thin black cheroot. He would clap enthusiastically, but he would never smile or show any other emotion. I found out some years later, that he was in fact a very good, and well known, artist, so my name for him was in fact, quite apt.

Paco Gumersindo has now left El Molino's, but he is certainly alive and well, and still singing, and can be heard occasionally in El Buro Blanco in Nerja, as well as La Posada Iberica, which is a small bar serving excellent tapas, in a small alleyway just off the far end of Calle Pintada.

Flamenco, of course, is not the only music you will hear in Nerja, the Spanish are well known for their love of music, dancing and singing, and this does include all types of music, from modern rock, to classical. In fact, during July and part of August, classical concerts, as well as many other types of music, performed by many top international entertainers, are held in the Caves of Nerja, where one of the enormous natural caverns is transformed into a concert hall.

The caves themselves, are of course, a wonderful site and a must for any visitor to Nerja, but to see a concert there is an unbelievable experience, which all the words I could write about it, could never express the sounds and the feelings one gets by actually being there, an experience you will have to see for yourself to fully appreciate.

Modern rock music is alive and certainly doing well in Nerja, as you will no doubt see and hear for yourself, if you have a television set while you are there, and switch on one of the local music channels, or alternatively, you could take a walk to the Plaza Tutti Frutti, and before you question this, yes, that is the correct name. The Plaza Tutti Frutti is a square in the centre of town, lined with bars, which only come to life, at night, and are inhabited not by Count Dracula and the undead, but by the youth of Nerja. Loud music? Yes. Aggressive behaviour? No. This is not to say that the occasional argument between a couple of youths will never happen, especially when there are so many pretty senoritas around, it is almost inevitable. But by nature, the Spanish are not an overtly aggressive race. They certainly make a lot of noise, reputedly one of the noisiest races in Europe, but for all their shouting and gesturing, these displays of manhood hardly ever go any further.

Unfortunately, where ever people of this age group gather in the world today, so we also find drugs, of one kind or another. This is not to say that Nerja has a flourishing drugs market, because it does not, but without beating about the bush, Spain as a whole, does! It is one of Europe's highest consumers of cocaine, cannabis and ecstasy. As far as cocaine is concerned, Spain has Europe's largest number of consumers. According to the statistics revealed by the Spanish Government last year, cocaine consumption among the Spanish population has doubled in the past 10 years.

The number of cannabis users is also rising and Spain, Denmark and the UK have the dubious honour of leading the European league of cannabis consumption. 36% of Spanish adolescents between 14 and 18, in other words 762,000 young people have consumed cannabis at some time in the past twelve months, this is double the consumption figure in Spain 10 years ago. Cannabis and cocaine are not the only problem, 27% of youngsters between 14 and 18 years of age admit to having got drunk in the past month, 31.8% more than 10 years ago, and consumption of new addictive substances such as liquid ecstasy is also on the rise. The only area in which Spain's National Drugs Plan seems to have been successful is in heroine consumption where figures show that the number of heroine addicts has actually gone down.

In my honest opinion, you can relax and forget about drugs while you are in Nerja, and if you are between 17 and 30, want a really good time, and do not have to get up too early the following morning, then Plaza Tutti Frutti might be just the place for you. If you are older than that, do not like a lot of noise, and have a young family with you, then I would suggest that you make sure before you stay in Nerja, that your hotel or apartment is not in that immediate area.

Nerja's street market, takes place every Tuesday in the area called Almijara, which is located on the eastern side of Nerja, just to the north of the Burriana Beach roundabout. The local council, in all its perceived wisdom, changed the location of the market a few years ago, from Chaparil, which is situated at the western side of the town, and used to stretch over many streets, and attracted thousands of visitors, to its new location, which only now attracts a fraction of the visitors.

You can still buy almost anything there, from clothing, to leather goods, to fruit and vegetables and other locally made produce. But the ambience and sounds of the old market are, I am afraid, long gone. I have noticed over the last 2 or 3 years, that the market stalls selling CDs are not nearly as busy as they used to be, when there was always a crowd around them. I do not think that this is due to falling interest in music, rather than to the gangs of mainly Senegalese, who now sell illegal copies, quite openly on almost every street, as well as in restaurants and bars. A legal CD or DVD, bought in a shop or on a market stall, usually costs between 10 and 15 Euros, whereas the Senegalese sell their illegal copies for 4 Euros each or 3 for 10 Euros. You can spot the illegal CD sellers a mile off, because they always carry their goods in Lidl Supermarket bags, and if I know that, you cannot tell me that the local police aren't aware of it?

The local attitude in Spain, and especially in Nerja, seems to be 'live and let live.' There is no racism, not that I have ever noticed anyhow. Bars and restaurants let almost anyone go in to sell their goods, from the CD boys, to carpet sellers, lottery salesmen, men selling fishing rods, and almost anything you can think of. I have often seen one of the CD boys asking the bar owner to change up a banknote for him, to allow him to give his customer change, and the bar owners do this without any fuss whatsoever, can you imagine the same thing happening in Britain? While I do believe this attitude can be a good one, I also believe that if an illegal activity is doing local businesses, like the music shops and stalls, out of their perfectly legal trade, then the police should do something about it.

As I have already said, there is no racism in Nerja, that I have ever noticed, but I am seriously worried, that unless something is done to curb the influx of illegal immigrants, who seem to mainly come from the African Continent, many of whom earn their living by selling illegal goods, then we could end up witnessing racism, which is so much against the Spanish nature, such as we have seen in other countries, like Germany, and more recently, France.

Spain's close proximity to Africa, does of course leave it wide open to invasion of one type or another from that continent. This started in 711 AD when the Moors first invaded and conquered Spain, and renamed it the Arabic name of Al Andalus, which is where we get the name Andalucia from today. The Moors reigned over Spain from 711 until 1492. In 1236 the Spanish Reconquista (Reconquest) which refers to the conquest by Christian kingdoms, mainly Castile, Len, Aragon and Portugal, of Muslim controlled areas in the Iberian Peninsula, taking place between 718 and 1492.
This led to the fall of the last Islamic stronghold of Granada under Mohammed ibn Alhamar to the Christian forces of Ferdinand 111 of Castile. From there on Granada became a vassal state to the Christian kingdom for the next 250 years until January 2nd 1492 when the last Muslim leader Boabdil of Granada surrendered complete control of the remnants of the last Moorish stronghold Granada, to Ferdinand and Isabella, Los Reyes Catlicos (The Catholic Monarchs).

Maybe it is the close proximity to the continent of Africa, and nearly eight hundred years of Moorish rule that has led Spain to become the tolerant nation that we see today. But feelings did change somewhat on 11th March 2004 when Islamic Terrorists killed 191 commuters in the Madrid Railway bombings. José María Aznar was the prime minister of Spain at the time, and had recently called for new elections to take place. Then, with just three days to go before the actual polling day, the Madrid bombings occurred, and evidence that was available and in accord with much of the press, the Aznar cabinet first blamed ETA, which had been caught trying to carry out an attack at Madrid's Chamartín train station the year before, and two weeks before that, several were detained carrying explosives like the ones used in the bombing.

As more evidence of Islamic involvement emerged two days after the Madrid bombings, demonstrations took place across Spain demanding news from the investigation, where chants such as "We want the truth before we vote" and "Who is responsible?" were heard.

All the evidence that started to come in, pointed to Islamic terrorists, but it seemed to take forever for Aznar to finally admit he was wrong, but after much pressure he finally switched blame away from ETA and onto the real culprits, Al-Qaida, but instead of giving the straight forward answer which people was calling for, he then said that the bombings were an attempt by Islamic extremists to reclaim Al Andalus, which they had been forced to abandon in 1492.

Three days after the train bombings, Aznar's PP Party, the People's party (Partido Popular) which is the largest liberal conservative political party in Spain. It defines itself as a centre party, lost the election to José Luis Rodriguez Zapatero's PSOE, the Spanish Socialist Workers' Party, commonly abbreviated by its Spanish initials, PSOE (Partido Socialista Obrero Español), but who were 12 seats short of an overall majority and this forced it into a loose coalition government with regional nationalist and left-wing parties. Certain PP representatives would continue to claim that there was a link between ETA and the March 11th bombing. Investigations held by a Parliamentary Committee were closed with no real results and the only opposition against closing it, from the PP.

The bombers were eventually discovered in the town of Leganes, when the police surrounded the building they were in and a gun battle took place. A Special Operations Squad was called in, but it was greeted by a huge explosion that blew down half the building, and killed one police officer. The bodies of seven terrorists were found in the rubble afterwards. They had blown themselves up with their own dynamite. It took experts several days to identify the men by the body parts and pieces that were found in the ruins of the building. All that was really found out, was that the men, all Moroccans, had very lose links to Al-Qaida, and were mainly petty crooks and drug dealers. As well as the body parts of the men involved, police also found a video tape, which they reconstructed, showing three of the men, dressed in white robes and heavily armed, declaring that Spain was Muslim by right and Christian only by force.

In the end, who had won? One hundred and ninety one innocent people had been murdered. A government had been thrown from office, a new government formed, and still no one had been convicted in a court of this terrible crime. The only thing that can be said with any certainty is that the majority of the people of Spain were changed, at least to a certain degree, that day. Nearly eight hundred years of living and coexisting peacefully, side by side with their Muslim neighbours, would never be quite the same again, not for many years anyway. Spain had played host to these people, and as I pointed out earlier, allowed them the freedom of their land, and all that goes with it, and in return they have been virtually spat upon. Let's just pray, to Gods of all nominations, that nothing of this nature happens again, for if it does, we could well see another uprising, this time a Christian one.

Chapter 5

As some of you might know, this book is an updated version of the original, which I wrote a few years ago. When I wrote the original, the law covering smoking in Spain, was much more lenient than it is now. In 2011 the Spanish Government passed a law prohibiting smoking in all indoor public places in Spain. The original law on smoking in Spain stated that if a premises was 100 square meters or less, then the owners could decide for themselves if they wished to allow smoking or not. Some bar owners either divided their premises into two distinct halves to get around this law, or closed half of it altogether, as it seemed to be more cost effective than loosing their smoking customers, whom, according to a recent poll, numbered between 80 and 90 percent of bar and restaurant customers in Spain. Recent figures showed that just 1% of all bars and restaurants in Spain decided to become anti smoking establishments.

This ruling worked perfectly well for many years, giving customers the choice of either smoking or non-smoking establishments, or at least sectioned off smoking and non-smoking establishments. As far as I could see, everyone was happy with the law as it stood, both smokers and non-smokers alike, they all had a fair choice.

When the new anti-smoking law came into existence this year, no one I spoke to could believe it. What for? They asked, everyone is happy with the way things are, but it happened nevertheless, and now, just as in the UK and many other countries, we have bars going out of business over it. Spain does have one over-riding factor, which helps them to survive this law, and that is their weather. In the colder countries such as the UK, smokers are forced out into the cold and rain to enjoy their habit, in Spain the weather permits a much more enjoyable experience, but there are still some bars that are suffering from this law, and they are the small bars that do not have any room outside to accommodate smokers. These are the bars that are now closing.

I remember in 2005 I visited what was then one of my favourite restaurants in Nerja, called El Nino, which also had a fine bar lining the length of the left hand side of the restaurant. The first thing I noticed were the no-smoking signs on the wall. At the end of the bar, stood the owner, who was the recent widow of the original owner, she was just along the bar from me, puffing away merrily on her cigarette. I laughed and asked her what that was all about, her smoking there by the bar, with a no smoking sign on the wall just behind her. I think she thought I was being serious at first, and she started showing me, that the no smoking signs were directed to one section of the restaurant only, where people could dine. From the bar, to the other dining end of the restaurant, anyone can smoke if they wish, she told me. Now this, is what I call live and let live! She went on to tell me, that she had only complied with the no smoking rule in that one area, because of the amount of British tourists, who complain about smoking. I did explain to her, that although I am British, in no way do I conform to this draconian ruling of taking people's freedom away from them.

Personally, I think that if non-smokers really do not want air polluted by tobacco smoke, they should eat in the open air, in the same manner that they love to force smokers to do. One final word on this subject, before I end up dedicating a whole chapter to it, and that is that I paid another visit to El Nino just a year after that visit, and I and sorry to say that they had then made the whole restaurant non smoking, and by the look of things there that evening, I would guess that they had also lost 40 to 50 percent of their customers at least, in doing so. Oh dear, I can feel that hobby-horse of mine galloping away with me again, I better have another cigarette before it gets out of control.

Forgetting smoking for a while, if you really enjoy good food and atmosphere, then El Nino is the place for you, it is a great looking place, very typically Spanish, with two dining areas, and a long bar in the centre. The staff are friendly, very efficient, and speak very good English, in fact the head waitress there, loves speaking English so much, that if you ask for anything in Spanish, like Cochinillo for instance, she will immediately say, 'yes, the suckling pig.' This is very nice of her, but not if you are trying to practise your Spanish. I suppose it does prove in one way, that you have pronounced it correctly, or she wouldn't have known what you were talking about enough to say it back to you in English would she? They do a starter, which consists of large prawns in a pastry shell, cooked in a white wine, cream and garlic sauce, which is absolutely out of this world, but be careful if you do have it, as it is also quite large and filling, and can tend to take your appetite away before you have even had your main course.

But I must admit, that the suckling pig in El Nino's is about the best I have tasted in Nerja. The only place where I have had better, is in a little village called Competa, which is about a 35 minute drive, up into the mountains above Torrox, which is just along the coast from Nerja. The restaurant in Competa where I had this is called Cortijo Paco. I ordered the Cochinillo the day before, from Paco, who is a very good friend of mine, and who is the owner of the restaurant. Just enough for my wife and myself, I told him, but when he brought it to our table, we had the whole restaurant looking on in amazement. It was the whole half of the pig, sliced right down the middle, from head to tail, complete with an apple in its mouth, a little curly tail and two tiny trotters. The meat was so white and succulent, that it almost melted in your mouth, and the crackling was just perfect. I must admit, I have never tasted anything as good as this before or since. And, we had so much that I took the dish over to some friends who were sitting nearby, and let them try some as well.

Although there is always a huge variety of fish dishes on the menus in nearly all the restaurants in Nerja and the nearby villages, meat, and especially game, also features prominently, but vegetarians should not be put off by this almost blatant display of meat on the menus, as almost all the restaurants in Nerja, as well as Paco's Restaurant in Competa of course, all do excellent varieties of vegetables, fish and rice, dishes, including Paella, where the ingredients can be changed to meet all tastes.

Getting back to El Nino's in Nerja, once again, as well as an excellent and varied menu, and daily specials, they also have a very large wine stock, and as I said earlier, a long bar, where you can have a drink while you are waiting, or if you feel like it, just go there for a drink, and maybe a few tapas, which, for those of you who do not know, are small dishes, sometimes consisting of just a few olives, or maybe a piece of tortilla (Spanish omelette), or a few gambas (prawns). These tapas are sometimes supplied free of charge with each drink that you buy.

In fact, if you know where to go, you can eat your way, completely free of charge, through enough tapas, during the course of an evening, that you won't have any need of a dinner. What you do need to bear in mind though, is that you will be doing an awful lot of drinking during that time. Personally, I think it's a lovely way to spend an evening!

To understand what Tapas are all about, is to get a little insight into the Spanish mentality and way of life. The word tapa means lid or a cover, and many years ago, when we didn't have the quality of hygiene that we have now, bars selling wine or beer, would place a plate, originally with just a piece of bread on it, which acted like a lid on top of the glass, to keep out the dirt, dust, and flies. Legend has it, that one enterprising bar owner decided to put a little cheese with the bread on the plate, and in doing so, he noticed a remarkable upturn in his business. As other bar owners got wind of his new found fortunes, so they too decided to add something extra to the plate, maybe a few olives, etc., and before you knew it, the tapa that we know today, was born.

Tapas can be grouped into three basic categories, cosas de picar, meaning basically, 'nibbles' which you can pick up, such as olives or peanuts. Pinchos, which are nearly always served on a stick or skewer, almost like a kebab, and lastly, Cazuelas, which is really the name of the little bowl shaped dish that these tapas are served in, which usually hold some kind of sauce, for example, albóndigas (meatballs) or prawns fried in garlic and chillies (gambas pil pil) There is an old Spanish proverb that states Comiendo el apetito se va abriendo. (appetite increases with constant eating) This might give you a better insight into what lies behind the culinary experience of Spain.

It is difficult to convey the excitement and liveliness of a tapas bar because they are not just about drinking wine and fine sherry, or eating free portions of food. A tapas bar is like a window into the Spanish soul and the Spanish gastronomic way of life. They are places where people of all classes and ages will congregate. Elegant men and beautiful women, scruffy students, fishermen, farmers, a tourist here and there, old folk and young, they are all inhabitants of the tapas bar. Their raucous conversation combined with the clatter of the plates and glasses as they are slammed down onto the bar, surrounds you, and seems to get louder and louder, as the evening wears on. Conversation about the bullfight, about football, politics, business deals, the lottery, and so it goes on, fine dry sherries, wine, and beer, drunk with countless tapas.

The tapas are a very characteristic part of the Spanish way of life that seems unlikely to be exported to other cultures, but have now become popular throughout the world. It not just about eating, or drinking, it is about the ability to bring together people from all walks of life, to gather, and to enjoy this informal ritual together, where eating standing up has become almost sacrosanct.

I was once at an outside bar in Almuñécar where they served tapas, when I noticed an elderly English couple come and seat themselves at a small table quite near to me. When their drinks arrived at their table, they were accompanied by two little tapas of arroz (rice), which is served up, very similar to paella, only much smaller portions of course. The woman turned to her husband and asked him if he had ordered this. He shook his head and told her that he definitely had not ordered it, and he told her not to touch it, 'once you even try it, they'll charge you for it' he said, and with that they both pushed the little dishes to the far side of their table, 'that'll show 'em'. I did dither a bit, on whether I should explain to them or not, about the tapas being free with their drinks, but in the end I decided against it, they would probably have told me that they were vegetarians or something similar, and started asking me if the rice contained meat extract or something as equally ridiculous.

One of the main problems, especially for people from Britain, is the fact that we just cannot believe that anyone would actually give us something for nothing. After all, if you buy a beer in the UK, that is what you get, a beer! The nearest thing I know in Britain, to free tapas, is in the east end of London, where pubs, on a Sunday morning, line their bars with free shellfish, such as prawns, cockles, whelks, and smoked herrings, which you can help yourself to until it has all gone, and believe me, this doesn't take very long, especially with customers like myself around. But not everyone in the UK has experienced the generosity of London's east end, and so they quite wrongly assume that the free dish of food upon their table is all a part of some elaborate scam. I sincerely hope that after reading this book, they will now understand, and be more enlightened as to the joys of free tapas in Spain.

For anyone who wants to try to cook a few tapas for themselves, or maybe just get an idea of what is on offer, here, following, are a few explanations and recipes:

Patatas Bravas (Fierce Potatoes)

INGREDIENTS 2 or 3 potatoes, Olive oil to fry, 3 medium full-grown tomatoes, 1 tsp. of Pimenton (spicy ground red pepper), Vinegar, 1 tsp. of flour, Salt.

Peel the potatoes and cut them into small pieces, then fry, on a low heat. Once cooked, drain the potatoes. Make the tomato sauce: Add a spoon of oil to the pan and then fry the deseeded and peeled tomatoes, smashing it. When cooked, add a few drops of vinegar, a teaspoon of flour and another teaspoon of the Pimenton (spicy ground pepper) and stir well to mix everything. Season and pour over the potatoes.

Calamares Fritos (Fried Squid)

INGREDIENTS 4 medium size squids, 1 glass of Flour, Salt, Olive oil, 1 Lemon.
Wash the squid well, removing all surface tissues. Tentacles have to be removed along with the innards, keeping only the tube shaped body. Sprinkle the squid with a little salt and coat with the flour. Shake off the excess flour. Fry them in deep very hot oil, then allow to rest on a paper serviette to drain off the oil. Served with lemon slices.

Tortilla (Potato Omelette)

INGREDIENTS 1/2 kg. Potatoes, 4 eggs, 1 Tbsp. olive oil, Salt.
Peel the potatoes and slice thinly. Cut the onion in very small pieces and add to the potatoes. Fry potatoes and onions in a generous amount of oil over a low heat, removing them with a palette knife when cooked and drain well. In a separate bowl, beat the eggs and mix with the potatoes. Leave for a few minutes so that the eggs fully absorb the potatoes.

Heat a pan with a Tbsp. of oil and then pour the mixture into the pan, over a low heat and let it thicken. Use a big flat dish or a lid to turn the mixture over and allow to cook on the other side.

Gambas a la plancha (Pan-grilled prawns)

INGREDIENTS 1/2 cup olive oil, Juice of 1 lemon, 2 teaspoons sea salt, 24 medium to large prawns, about 1 pound in weight, in their shells with heads intact.

In a bowl, whisk together the olive oil, lemon juice, and salt until well blended. Dip the prawns briefly into the mixture to coat lightly. Heat a dry skillet over high heat. When the pan is very hot, working in batches, add the prawns in a single layer without crowding. Sear for 1 minute. Decrease the heat to medium and continue cooking for 1 minute longer. Turn the prawns, increase the heat to high, and sear for 2 more minutes, or until golden. Keep the prawns warm on an ovenproof plate in a low oven. Cook the rest of the prawns in the same way.

When all the prawns are cooked, arrange on a serving dish and serve immediately.

Riñones al Jerez (Kidneys in Sherry)

INGREDIENTS 10 fresh lambs' kidneys, 1 big onion, chopped, 4 tablespoons olive oil, 4 oz bacon, 1 garlic clove, finely chopped, 2 tablespoon flour, 4 fl. oz fino Sherry or Montilla, 1 tablespoon tomato concentrate, 2 sprigs fresh thyme, Salt and freshly ground black pepper.

Fry the onion in 2 tablespoons of oil over a low heat in a big frying pan. When it starts to soften add the diced bacon and garlic. Remove the membranes and cut out the middle cores from the kidneys, then cut them into large dices.

Remove and reserve the onion and bacon from the pan and add 1-2 tablespoons more olive oil. Put in the diced kidneys, a handful at a time, over the highest heat and stir occasionally. When they are sealed, pull them to the sides of the pan and add the next handful. When they are all sealed and coloured, return the onions and bacon, sprinkle with flour and stir in.
Add the Fino, tomato concentrate and thyme and bring to a simmer. Season to taste.

Champinones al ajillo (mushrooms in garlic)

INGREDIENTS 1 lb (450g) mushrooms, 2 oz (55g) pine nuts, 1 lemon, 2 garlic cloves (finely chopped), 4 Tblsp dry sherry, 4 Tblsp olive oil, salt and ground black pepper, parsley.

Heat some olive oil in a large frying pan. Add the chopped garlic and cook until the garlic is light brown. Add the sliced mushrooms, pine nuts and the sherry and cook for about 3 minutes, turning frequently. Now add the juice of the lemon and the chopped parsley, a pinch of salt and some ground pepper. Stir and serve hot.

Albondigas (meat balls in tomato sauce)

INGREDIENTS 500g minced beef, 3-4 cloves garlic, 1 onion, parsley, 1 egg (beaten), 4 tomatoes, roughly chopped, 2 slices stale bread, milk, white wine, flour, salt, pepper, olive oil.

In a blender or mortar, crush 2 cloves of garlic with the parsley and mix with a dash of white wine. Place this mixture in a large bowl with the mince, mix well and then leave to stand for 20 minutes. Place the bread in a shallow dish and cover with the milk. Leave to soak for a few minutes. Add the bread, egg, salt and pepper to the mince and knead until all the ingredients are mixed together. Make small balls and roll each one in flour, then cook in plenty of hot oil until they turn golden brown, drain and place in a casserole dish. For the sauce: Finely chop the onion and the remaining garlic using a little oil from the meatballs, gently fry the onion and garlic until they begin to brown. Add the chopped tomatoes and about half a glass of white wine. Bring to the boil and cook for 5 minutes. Pour the sauce over the meatballs and then place in a moderate oven for 20 - 25 minutes.

Chapter 6

Nerja, was not always the sophisticated resort that we see today. If you go back just a relatively few years, to the nineteen fifties for instance, it was still a small village that relied almost entirely on fishing and a little farming. The restaurants that you see in abundance today, just did not exist back then, and there was no foreseeable reason why they should have, with no tourist trade to speak of. One man however, thought differently, his name was Miguel.

Until a few years ago, Miguel owned and ran a very fine restaurant in the very centre of Nerja, at the corner of Calle Pintada and Almirante. The restaurant was named after him, Miguel's. I used to eat at Miguel's quite often, and the milk fed lamb he served, was second to none. Over the years I got to know him and his wife quite well, and would often see them both, making their way home after the restaurant was closed, often about one o'clock in the morning. I was having a meal there one evening when Miguel told me that he was closing the restaurant within the next couple of weeks. I was so shocked, as I had come to view Miguel's as part of Nerja's tradition and history. I asked him what he was going to do, was he about to retire maybe? Miguel frowned at the thought of retiring, middle aged he might be, but retiring age, never! It wasn't a word in his vocabulary. As was his custom, he brought the usual bottle of his best Brandy to my table and poured me a large glass. I invited him to sit down and join me, as it was closing time anyway. So as we toasted each other with his fine Brandy, he started to tell me about how he came to start his restaurant there.

He came from a large family, and was brought up in a small house in the nearby village of Maro, which is the little village next to Nerja. His parents worked all their lives on their small plot of land, just about managing to scrape a bare living in order to keep the family. But no matter how hard they worked, there was never enough for them to get out of the poverty trap which most fishing villages in Spain suffered at that time. Miguel looked around him, and at the nearby towns of Torremolinos and Malaga, he saw the beginning of tourism starting to take off in those places, and he knew that it wouldn't be very long before it actually hit Nerja also, and so, armed with his foresight, he saved everything he could and eventually opened his restaurant in Nerja in the mid sixties.

It was a tremendous risk of course, as Nerja, at that time was still only just starting to attract tourists, there were one or two hotels, and a few apartment blocks, but restaurants, of the type Miguel eventually opened, were far and few between, so here he was taking the biggest gamble of his life, knowing that if his predictions didn't come to fruition, both he and his family would be even worse off than when he was a child. But, he wanted his children to have a better life than he had. Tourists, he said, need two main things, somewhere to stay, and somewhere to eat. His judgement and predictions proved accurate and his restaurant flourished as the tourist trade started to take off.

So why, I asked him, after all these years of running one of the most successful restaurants in Nerja, was he finally giving it up to start a shop of all things? He smiled as he poured me another glass of Brandy. 'The most important thing in our lives, is our children' he told me, which I whole-heartedly agree with. 'And do you know what?' He said, 'since my children were born, I can count on one hand, the number of times I have sat down to dinner with them, even at Christmas time, both my wife and I are always working in the restaurant, I hardly ever get the time to even talk to them'. I could see Miguel's face looking sadder as he spoke; this was obviously a very hard decision for him. 'If I stay here another few years,' he said, 'they will be grown up and I will have lost so much, and then what would I have to show for a lifetime's work?' 'Money in the bank certainly, but at the expense of the most important thing in everyone's lives, our families!'

You sometimes hear some locals (not many) in Nerja complaining about how much it has changed there, and how better the old days were, but not Miguel, he thanks the tourism industry for giving him the chance to earn the sort of money that his father and family before him could only have dreamed of. Miguel closed the restaurant and opened La Tienda de

Miguel, a shop on the same site, selling all types of fine foods and wines, similar in fact to what he sold at his restaurant, but with much more sociable and family orientated hours. La Tienda only lasted a couple of years, and Miguel turned it into a tobacco shop, offering goods at almost wholesale prices. His new tobacco shop seems to be doing very well, as contrary to what one hears, smoking in Spain is still a very popular past-time, and tourist still flock to stock up before returning home, where cigarettes and tobacco are at least double the price. In the last year however, Spain have introduced a very draconian smoking-ban, which I sincerely hope will not affect Miguel's business, as it has affected businesses in the UK.

Stop-Press: I have just heard that Miguel has sold his tobacco business, and much to his old restaurant clientel's delight, has recently opened another restaurant, called Plaza del del Olvido Restaurante which is in a charming square just at the corner of Calle Los Huertos and Calle Frigiliana.

The Nerja of the 1950s and before, which Miguel described, is hard to conceive for the ordinary tourist visiting there today. The beautiful beaches didn't have tourists sunbathing on them, under brightly coloured sun-shades. The beaches then, were places of work, filled with fishing boats, and men who looked much older than their years, forever mending their nets, and bringing their paltry little catches of fish, usually sardines, in from their small boats, to be sold on the quayside for a few pesetas, to hopefully see them through to the next day, and so it was almost every day, living from hand to mouth for most people at that time. There wasn't any government or European subsidies to be handed out to the fishing industry, as it is today, nor to the farmers, and there certainly wasn't any social services, which would help the poor and needy, these people were left to fend for themselves, make a go of it or starve, that was their options.

Even the centre of Nerja was unrecognisable from what it is today. There were of course some shops and bars in the town, but these were mainly shops that sold groceries and other every day household goods, and the bars were no more than just small houses, with a wooden bar erected in the living room, and a couple of barrels of locally made wine, stacked on a shelf at the back. Other than this, the ordinary houses were usually small and run down, and the streets themselves were mostly just dirt tracks.

I have seen old black and white photos of what Nerja was like in those days, and in most cases, I have needed the help of someone local, usually an older person, to explain exactly what area we are looking at. The church of course, is instantly recognisable, even if the immediate surroundings are not.

As I have said previously, Nerja is not just about Spanish people, and the more it has developed, so the more cosmopolitan it has become, with people from almost every country in the world now settling there. But when one wants to know something about the old days in Nerja, you would think that an old or elderly, local would be the most knowledgeable person on the subject, so you will probably appreciate how astounded I was, when a centenarian American woman, whom I met in a bar in town one night, started giving me lessons on the history of Nerja.

This woman, who will remain nameless, was apparently part of a very well know American family, and, so the story went, was also immensely rich. I saw her come into the bar on the arm of a man, some years her junior, I never did find out what the exact relationship was between them, not that it particularly mattered. She was very frail and the man had to help her to one of the stools at the bar. At first glance, she certainly looked elderly, but definitely not ancient, and I was really shocked when I was told that she was reputedly 100 years old. If I remember correctly, I think her drink was Canadian Club, on the rocks, which she apparently drunk, every night, just the one per night, of course.

She was certainly a character, and she knew it, and played upon it, holding court, and engaging other customers in long bouts of conversation, as if she were the Queen of Nerja. As the night wore on and customers started to drift away, I suddenly found myself in closer proximity to her, and it was only when this close, that I could see through the pancake of makeup and the enormous sun glasses, that it was Posh Becks, only a joke of course, what I could really see was the real age of this ancient woman.

I think that someone mentioned that I had something to do with properties there in Nerja, and with that, the Queen of Nerja honoured me with her attention. 'Do you live here in Nerja?' she enquired, 'where exactly is your house?'. I told her that the properties I dealt in were not mine, that I just acted as an agent for properties to let in Nerja. I don't think she even heard my answer, or if she did, she certainly didn't pay much attention to it. She told me that she lived in a big house in this same street where the bar was situated. This particular street is one of the most expensive in Nerja, and known locally as Millionaire's row. I also heard later that she owns many houses, some in Nerja, some in other parts of Spain, and others in the USA. So all in all the old girl was quite well stashed, to say the least.

She told me that she had been living there since 1952, 'do you know this street?' She said, 'when I first moved here it was just a dirt track with fisherman's cottages each side, I could have bought the whole street for the price of a second-hand car today'. I feigned interest and offered her another drink, which she immediately declined with a dismissive wave of her hand. 'And you know what else? I met my first Spanish lover on this street also, how about that?' I embarrassingly smiled and took another swig of my drink. 'But that wasn't the last' she said, 'not by a long chalk, and they haven't all been just Spanish either'. The man with her, glanced round at her as she said this, a slightly worried look upon his face, as if to ask 'oh no, what's she going to say next?' 'Well' she said, 'time to leave I guess, you did say you lived near here didn't you, who knows, maybe I'll meet my lucky number 69 tonight huh?'

The man with her quickly got her to her feet and guided her out of the bar as quickly and quietly as he could, with her turning to flash her enormous set of overwhite dentures at me as she headed out the door. I have had some history lessons in my life, but never one like this before. This was the sort of story that you hear in bars all over the world, but this wasn't just a story, it was true, and the last I heard, the old girl was still alive and well, and as far as I know, still frequenting bars, and hoping to meet her lucky number 69 before time runs out on her.

Apart from the obvious beauty of Nerja, its beaches, coastline, tropical plants and wonderful climate, the other thing that makes Nerja work so well for the holiday maker and inhabitants alike, is its businesses, and the way they are run. It is business which, originally brought tourism to Nerja, and it is business, with its thoroughly modern approach to tourism that keeps Nerja one step ahead of its rivals along the coast. Over the years many businesses have come and gone in Nerja, from bars and restaurants to estate agents and shops. The vast majority of businesses in Nerja, are Spanish owned, but there are still quite a few foreign owned businesses, mostly from the European countries, which do include English.

I must say, that out of all the Spanish businesses that I know and have dealt with in one way or another, at least 99% of them are thoroughly nice, honest, and polite people, who give you exactly what they say they are going to give you. If you go into the smallest and cheapest little bar or cafe in Nerja, you will find the rich Spanish businessman, happily standing next to a local farmer, enjoying their coffee together. But I am afraid that I cannot say the same for the majority of the non-Spanish, especially the English, which is such a shame, as I am English myself. Snobbery has always been something that I could not stand, and although there are many non-Spanish inhabitants in Nerja, who are thoroughly nice people, and fit into the Spanish way of life without any problems, there is always the exception.

One such person, is an Englishman whom I will not name, but he runs a business in Nerja, and can speak reasonably good Spanish, which I think he rightly should do, if he lives and works there, and does business with Spanish people. I knew this man, and got on quite well with him for a number of years, but then I started to notice, that every time I saw him, so his head had grown a little bit bigger. He couldn't wear ordinary trousers and shirts any more; he could now only wear trousers or shirts with designer labels on them. Nothing particularly wrong with this you might think, that is unless you talk about almost nothing else, and brag incessantly about how much they cost as well.

One afternoon I met him at a local cafe, where he always stopped for coffee, and the first thing I noticed about him, was his stance, the way he waved me to a seat without actually saying anything. The next, was the way he answered his mobile phone, not with his name or his number, or even a brief hello, but 'talk to me.' I couldn't believe this, who did this guy think he was? I tried telling myself that maybe he had had a bad night, or a deal had fallen through, but later, when he invited me to see his new office, which was in a brand new building, right on the sea front, I realised that his head had become so swollen, that he had lost touch with reality. He had an enormous carved desk that was perched on a raised platform, to give him added height over anyone that came to see him. But the real eye opener was his chair behind the desk, it wasn't just a chair, it was a throne, a huge carved throne. I think he had been seeing too many gangster movies. I have never seen a Spanish businessman act like this, and I have known some of the most successful in Nerja.

Before I go any further, I would like to point out that I am not in the business of running the British down just for the sake of it, but I do think that if British businesses in Spain are giving our country a bad name, then it is only right that someone should speak out against them. I would like to name them, but obviously cannot for legal reasons.

The second British run business, which I thought was run appallingly, was an estate agent's office in Nerja, quite a big chain actually. I went there one day on behalf of a friend in the UK who was looking for a cheap property to buy somewhere along the coast. I had phoned my friend and told him about a property I had seen advertised by this particular agency, and my friend had asked me if I wouldn't mind going to view it for him. I telephoned the agent in Nerja and spoke to one of the staff there, who then arranged an appointment for me to view the property the following morning.

I turned up promptly at 09.30 sharp, to be greeted by two large Alsatian dogs, running around lose, in an office, which was obviously in the process of moving. After sitting there for ten to fifteen minutes I was eventually asked by someone, what did I want? I told this person, who said that they were very busy as they were moving that day, but they would pass me onto the boss, who would be happy to deal with me. When the boss, the Englishman who also happened to own the two dogs, finally deemed to give me an audience, the first thing he asked me, was what property was I talking about, and when he found out that it was just some cheap property down the coast, he was decidedly off. 'Did you book an appointment for this morning?' he snapped, I told him that I thought I had, to which he replied, 'thought, what do you mean you thought, either you did or you didn't?'. I was just so angry with this conceited idiot, that I walked out, telling him before I left that I wouldn't dream of doing business with his company, and that I would certainly tell everyone I knew, not to deal with them either. Two British owned businesses, both run by egomaniacs, not a lot I know, but in my opinion, two too many.

Chapter 7

The Spanish, as a race, are often given very negative publicity, when it comes to animals and their supposed treatment of them. We hear of ceremonies where goats are apparently thrown from towers, plus of course, the most famous, or infamous, depending on your particular tastes, the bullfight, which many northern Europeans seem to find so distasteful.

The inhabitants of Nerja, as far as I am aware, indulge in neither of these activities, but in order for you to try to understand the Spanish mentality, a little history of what is actually involved regarding animals and their treatment in Spain, would I think, be of some benefit to anyone interested in the culture of Spain.

The "goat throwing" tradition, which I am sure many of you may have heard of, takes place annually in a small village called Manganeses de la Polvorosa, in the northwest of Spain, above Madrid. It is held on the fourth Sunday in January every year, in honour of its patron saint, St Vincent. On this day, a group of young men from the village go out and round up one of the local goats. The goat is then carried along in a crowded procession to the church at the centre of the village, and up into the bell tower of the church, where it is then thrown, some 15 meters, approximately 50 feet, down into a waiting sheet of tarpaulin, which is held open by the cheering crowd below.

According to Manganeses' 890 residents, this ancient ritual has been going on for as long as anyone can remember. It started, so they say, with a local priest there, who once owned a rather special goat. The Padre would often travel around the village, and the immediate countryside, and miraculously feed the poor and the destitute with the milk from his goat. One day, however, the beloved goat wandered into the church's bell tower, and when the bell rang out for Sunday mass, the poor creature became frightened, and leapt from the tower, hurtling towards the street below. Luckily, a group of locals had seen the frightened creature in the tower, and had anticipated what it was going to do, and so the goat was caught with a blanket and saved by the villagers. What I am trying to point out here, is that far from being the act of cruelty to animals, that many people perceive this to be, it is in fact re-enacted at the beginning of this festival to celebrate and to honour the loving priest and his goat, and the villagers that saved it.

Bullfighting, is totally different, and contrary to many people's beliefs, it is not regarded as a sport in Spain, but as an art. You will not find reference to Bullfighting on the back pages of newspapers, alongside football, but in the culture sections of the papers. If you have never seen a bullfight, or corridas de toros, here is a brief description of what actually happens, so that you can make up your own mind whether you want to see one while you are in Spain.

One afternoon's corrida involves six bulls, to be killed by three matadors, each encounter lasting about 15 minutes. At the appointed time, usually 5 PM, the three matadors, each followed by their assistants, the banderilleros, and the picadors, march into the ring to the accompaniment of traditional paso doble music, played by a live band. The matadors are the stars of the show, in their distinctive costumes, consisting of a silk jacket heavily embroidered in gold, skin-tight trousers, and a montera (a bicorne hat). A traje de luces (suit of lights), can cost several thousand pounds; a top matador must have at least six of them a season.

When a bull first comes into the arena out of the toril, or bull pen gate, the matador greets it with a series of manoeuvres, or passes, with a large cape; these passes are usually verónicas, the basic cape manoeuvre (named after the woman who held out a cloth to Christ on his way to the crucifixion).

The amount of applause the matador receives is based on his proximity to the horns of the bull, his tranquillity in the face of danger, and his grace in swinging the cape in front of an infuriated animal weighing more than 460 kg (1,000 lb). The bull instinctively goes for the cloth because it is a large, moving target, not because of its colour; bulls are colour-blind and charge just as readily at the inside of the cape, which is yellow.

Fighting bulls charge instantly at anything that moves because of their natural instinct and centuries of special breeding. Unlike domestic bulls, they do not have to be trained to charge, nor are they starved or tortured to make them savage. Those animals selected for the corrida are allowed to live a year longer than those assigned to the slaughterhouse.

Bulls to be fought by novilleros (novices) are supposed to be three years old and those fought by full matadors are supposed to be at least four years old.

The second part of the corrida consists of the work of the picadors, bearing lances and mounted on horses (padded in compliance with a ruling passed in 1930 and therefore rarely injured). The picadors wear flat-brimmed, beige felt hats called castoreños, silver-embroidered jackets, chamois trousers, and steel leg armour. After three lancings or less, depending on the judgement of the president of the corrida for that day, a trumpet blows, and the banderilleros, working on foot, advance to place their banderillas (brightly adorned, barbed sticks) in the bull's shoulders in order to lower its head for the eventual kill. They wear costumes similar to those of their matadors but their jackets and trousers are embroidered in silver.

After the placing of the banderillas, a trumpet sounds signalling the last phase of the fight. Although the bull has been weakened and slowed, it has also become warier, and in some cases, angrier, during the course of the fight, sensing that behind the cape is its true enemy; most gorings occur at this time. The heavy serge cloth of the muleta (small red cape) is draped over the estoque, (curved sword used for killing the bull) and the matador begins what is called the faena, the last act of the bullfight. The aficionados (ardent fans) study the matador's every move; the ballet-like passes practised since childhood. (Most matadors come from bullfighting families and learn their art when very young.) As with every manoeuvre in the ring, the emphasis is on the ability to increase but control the personal danger, maintaining the balance between suicide and mere survival.

In other words, the real contest is not between the matador and an animal; it is the matador's internal struggle.

The basic muleta passes are the trincherazo, generally done with one knee on the ground and at the beginning of the faena; the pase de la firma, simply moving the cloth in front of the bull's nose while the fighter remains motionless; the manoletina, a pass invented by the great Spanish matador Manolete (Manuel Laureano Rodríguez Sánchez), where the muleta is held behind the body; and the natural, a pass in which danger to the matador is increased by taking the sword out of the muleta, thereby reducing the target size and tempting the bull to charge at the larger object—the bullfighter.

After several minutes spent in making these passes, wherein the matador tries to stimulate the excitement of the crowd by working closer and closer to the horns, the fighter takes the sword and lines up the bull for the kill. The blade must go between the shoulder blades; because the space between them is very small, it is imperative that the front feet of the bull be together as the matador hurtles over the horns. The kill, properly done by aiming straight over the bull's horns and plunging the sword between its withers into the aorta region, requires discipline, training, and raw courage; for this reason it is known as the moment of truth.

I hope that I have demonstrated here, that neither of the aforementioned spectacles are concerned in any way, with deliberate cruelty to animals. The first, being concerned with a religious ceremony, giving thanks to man and animal, and the second, being almost like a religious celebration of man's bravery, skill, and dominance over the beast within us all.

When I was quite young, I was crossing a field once, with a friend, and we were suddenly charged, by a herd of cows, not ferocious bulls, just ordinary domestic cows. My friend told me that if we turned to face them and made loud noises at them, that they would run away and leave us alone. This was just rubbish, as nothing stopped those charging beasts, except for the fence that we just managed to get to in time and scramble over before they reached us. I shudder to think what injuries they would have caused to us, two young boys, if they had caught us. So please don't let anyone tell you that these animals are passive, and that it is only humans that are the aggressors.

Chapter 8

Malaga

The nearest Plaza de Toros to Nerja, is in Malaga, which is only about a 30 minute drive away. It is a beautiful, and old building, and well worth a visit, even if you are not planning on watching an actual bullfight. The bullring also houses a museum of bullfighting, which again is very interesting, and houses details and pictures of many famous bullfighters, as well as some of their blood splattered clothes, and the mounted heads of some of the bravest bulls.

A few years ago I paid the museum a visit, and whilst there, my wife took a photo of me looking straight into the eyes of one of the mounted bull's heads. I must admit that the thing that struck me the most about the bull's head, was the enormous size of it. The cows I had encountered as a child, were mere kittens compared to this. As I stared into its now glass eyes, I imagined for a few brief moments, what it must be like to have to stand face to face with this beast when it was alive, to feel its hot breath on your face, and to see its horns, poised, ready to impale you. Some people say that the bull doesn't stand a chance. I beg to differ, I think the bull stands every chance of killing the man, or at the least, severely injuring him, and in my opinion, it takes a very special, and very brave man, to face this sort of danger.

A funny side to my visit to the museum of bullfighting, was when I returned to the UK and showed the picture of me facing the bull's head, to my elderly mother, whose eyes were then starting to fail her, she stared at the picture for a while and then turned to my wife and said, 'Isn't my Pete brave, standing so close to that bull'. We did all laugh when we told her that it was only a bull's head mounted on a plaque, but I often think of that, when I hear people who have never seen a real bullfight, saying that they think it is cruel and should be stopped. I have even heard of people who cheer when they learn that a bullfighter has been gored. I say, go and see a bullfight for yourself, before you condemn it, and then ask yourself, could you face a ferocious charging animal like that?

The vast majority of Spanish people that I know have a very high regard for animals. In fact, you will see more people out walking their pet dogs in Nerja and the nearby towns, than you ever do in the UK. But, they also seem to have a need to show who is the master when it comes to man and beast. One businessman, whom I work with in Nerja, regularly visits Scotland on hunting and fishing trips. Whilst another, who I know, who owns a marisqueria (fish restaurant) just along the coast from Nerja, in Torre Del Mar, has a large selection of photos, proudly displayed in the bar, of himself with his son, also on a hunting trip, complete with their rifles, in snow bound northern Spain. These are proud men, proud of their skills, their country, and traditions, and their manhood.

Spain seems to be losing so many of it ancient traditions since Zapatero became prime minister, and gaining in their place, so much of the mundane ways and so called modernisation projects, which the European Union has already imposed upon the rest of Europe. I just hope that an effective opposition party manages to reign him in somewhat before the damage being done becomes irreparable.

Malaga, isn't just about the bullring, and neither is it, just the city that happens to share the name of the nearest airport to Nerja either. Malaga City is only a 30-minute drive away from Nerja, or you can get there by bus from the centre of Nerja.

Málaga is the major coastal city of Andalucia and is a genuine and typical Andaluz city with a gritty individualism mainly untouched by tourism and, to a large extent, the passage of time.

The Moors occupied the city until the mid fifteenth century, after which it grew to become one of the foremost merchant centres in the entire Iberian Peninsula. This illustrious past has left its imprint on the historic centre, particularly around La Alcazaba, a fortress that dates back to 1065 and is now a fascinating archaeological museum.

If you are walking around Malaga, La Alcazaba sits up high on a cliff top above you, close to the tunnel that links the docks and the park area, with the old part of the city. Close to the Alcazaba is the castle that was rebuilt by the Moors and is today a traditional parador (state run hotel) with superb panoramic views. During the nineteenth century, Málaga was a popular winter resort for the wealthy, famed for its elegance and sophistication. The impressive park on Calle Alameda dates back to this era and is recognised as being one of the most celebrated botanical collections in Europe. During the winter, open-air concerts are held here every Sunday that makes a refreshing change from the bucket and spade scenario on the coast.

Pablo Picasso is the city's famous son (not forgetting Antonio Banderas of course) and there are several galleries showing Picasso's work, including the 16th century Museum of Fine Arts, adjacent to the Cathedral. His birthplace in Plaza Merced is today an archive of his life and works and open to the public; the entrance is absolutely free (so are all the services: Documentation Centre, exhibitions, museum, and video projections).

Málaga's main theatre is the Teatro Cervantes, where Antonio Banderas once trod the boards, and still pays occasional visits.

As well as being a cultural centre, Malaga is also a great place to eat out. The Malagueños love their food and the bars and restaurants here are where the real social life takes place. The choice is unlimited and, on the whole, reasonable with some bars offering a menu of the day with bread and wine for as little as 8 or 9 Euros. They also serve a variety of tapas of course. The best known local fare in Malaga is Pescaito Frito, an assortment of fried fish, including small sardines and red mullet, best washed down with a glass of ice cold fino at one of the many old fashioned bodegas in town. But it is El Palo, to the east of the city that is a typical fisherman's village and the place to go if you want that veritable "catch of the day" freshness.

My particular favourite tapas bar in Malaga is El Pimpi. Everybody who is anybody has been to El Pimpi. Bullfighter 'El Cordobes,' the sixties heartthrob known in his time as the 'Beatle of the bullring.' Film star Antonio Banderas is a regular visitor, his family still live in the town. And the King himself, Don Juan Carlos who, arriving with Queen Sofia in the Royal Yacht to open the adjacent Picasso Museum on a particularly wet day, popped in to escape the rain.

Housed in the historic building that began life as a convent, El Pimpi oozes authentic Andulucian charm. The present owner, Don Francisco Campos, plans to keep it that way. A distinguished septuagenarian, he has owned the establishment since the early 1960s when the tourist boom was just beginning. Things were very different then.

'When I came to Malaga in the 1950s there were at least half a dozen locales like this' he explains. 'One by one they've been modernised; now we are the only one left. The last example of the traditional taverna.'

Everything about El Pimpi smacks of the traditional, right down to the double entrance, the front is in Calle Granada, just off the Plaza Merced, the back opposite the Albeniz cinema and the Roman amphitheatre in the Calla Alcazabilla. In more lawless times, this set up allowed the less honest elements of society to beat a hasty retreat at the approach of enraged creditors in pursuit of payment that was being squandered on wine, women and song. Nowadays the clientele is slightly more salubrious and ranges from students in their twenties through extended families to members of the Malaguenean smart set.

As for the name, the dictionary definition lists a Pimpi as "a woodland sprite", But in local dialect, it was the title given to young lads who used to sell trinkets to visiting sailors or cruise passengers, darting like imps between liners and merchant shipping, hawking their wares from small skiffs.

Inside the atmosphere is heavily Andalucian, from the bull's head in the entrance hall, to the original azulejos (the blue and white wall-tiles), to the uneven stone floors. Climbing plants cover the ceiling of the indoor patio. Barrels of Malaga wine line the main seating area. There is even a 'tertulia' room where Malaga's creative element- artists, writers, actors and painters- hold regular soirees. And in May the entrance hall exhibits a May Cross, constructed entirely from flowers. A tribute to the coming of spring that dates back to a pagan past.

The building itself is surprisingly large, opening up and back from a deceptively narrow doorway in Calle Granada, next to 'Entrecuadros' a chi- chi boutique selling deliciously collectable objets d'arte, into an entrance hall, welcomingly cool on a hot Summer's evening. Upstairs, the long bar is covered with signed photographs of famous stars and high society members who have enjoyed Don Francisco's hospitality. Everyone from Paloma Picasso, the artist's jewellery- designing daughter, to the Duchess of Alba, whose ancestries posed nude for Goya's painting "The Naked Maja" has visited. The Duchess holds more than 40 titles, glories in the name Caeyatana Fitz-James Stewart and reputedly has more blue blood in her veins than all the crowned heads of Europe put together. Tucked on a wall opposite the long bar, amongst all these portraits of the great and the good is a shot of a very young, Tony Blair, grinning, as usual, like Cheshire cat.

On a visit, a few years back, when Mr Blair was still the British Prime Minister, I sat at the bar, directly opposite his picture, and watched as everyone who came in, paused at the various pictures, pointing to those they recognised. I was quite amused by the fact that not one person seemed to recognise our grinning premier, until one small boy came along. He pointed to the picture, and then turned to his parents, who were following up behind him, 'who does he play for?' He asked in his British accent, his father prodded him along, and replied 'how would I know, I've never seen him before'. I had to smile to myself as I wondered how the "great man himself" would have felt if he had heard that?

The indoor patio boasts a small but quaint area of half a dozen tables and a tiny drinking fountain. Upstairs is the Palomar, where most of the cultural offerings of the sala take place. El Pimpi has always been famous for its flamenco, and unlike many other places in the region, they still offer the genuine article, as opposed to the type watered down for tourist consumption.

A cosy room lined with barrels and decorated with bullfight posters dating from the turn of the last century forms the main body of the downstairs level. This area holds about 60 people when it's full, which is the case most evenings from 10pm onwards.

Although not a restaurant El Pimpi does offer tapas. Tablas (round wooden platters) of ham, cheese and chorizo cost between 8 to 10 Euros. Other tasty snacks include ligeritos, oval rolls stuffed with an inventive variety of fillings, pringa (meat, ham and black pudding), and Campesino (avocado and anchovies) all served with crunchy 'patatas.' So, a perfect place to start or end the evening, or to pop into at any time of the day should the mood take you. I cannot ever pass it without paying a visit.

These days, Málaga prides itself on being a modern city with the heart of commerce dominated by Calle Larios that is the local Bond Street equivalent. This is the recommended place to start exploring the city as it is surrounded by attractive small streets and plazas, as well as the magnificent renaissance cathedral with its baroque façade and choir by Pedro de Mena. There are daily guided tours of the cathedral, and when you are finished there, you might like to visit the wonderful cafe, with its outside seating, which is in the narrow alleyway that runs beside the cathedral. This cafe dates back to the early 1900s, and its decor hasn't been changed during all that time. All in all, Malaga is a great city, and well worth staying there for at least for a night or two to get the true feel of it.

Chapter 9

Another of the really good things about Nerja, is its easy accessibility to other towns and villages, and with the new motorway, (E15) already linking Nerja to Malaga and beyond that to Marbella and Torremolinos, the journey times are now cut down considerably. At the time of writing, the E15 now reaches to the outskirts of Almuñécarr, although you still need to cut off and head back down to the old coastal road, and drive the last few miles into .Almunecar town.

Personally, I actually love driving along the old winding coastal road, the N340 from Nerja towards Almuñécarr, the scenery is absolutely breathtaking, though not for the faint hearted, with the magnificent peaks of the Sierra de Almijaras on your left, and the steep cliffs leading down to the beautiful Mediterranean on your right. And believe me, the bends of this particular stretch of road, are really hairpin shaped, so tight some of them, that all you can hear are your tyres screeching as you grip your steering wheel tightly and manoeuvre the bends. You really do need to keep your wits about you, and your eyes on the road. There are several stopping points along this road, to allow drivers to pull in and have a rest and take photos of the marvellous scenery. From these viewpoints you can see the motorway sitting high above you, as it cuts its way through the mountains, resting on huge concrete stilts. I remember seeing these enormous concrete pillars, lying beside the roadside, before they were hoisted into position. How they ever got them up there, and laid the road on top of them I don't know, but is must have taken a marvellous feet of engineering skill to do so, and I did read that quite a few of the workers died in the process. If you are in a hurry, then these motorways are marvellous, but if, like myself, you just want to relax, and see as much of the scenery as possible, then I would suggest that you carry on using the old N340.

Maro

Using this road, heading eastwards from Nerja, you come first to Maro, which is a really nice, picturesque, little village, with just a few shops, restaurants and bars. There is also a nice church there and one hotel. It always reminds me of a scene from one of those old Western Movies, where the hero rides in on his horse and ties it to a hitching post outside the only saloon in town. A piece of tumbleweed blows across the street, and a lone face peers out from a window across the way, 'looks like we got us a stranger in town' they say.

If you want real peace and solitude, you will definitely find it here, so long as you are not planning to rob the local saloon that is.

La Herradura

A further 20 minutes drive along the coast, brings you to a somewhat larger town called La Herradura, which means the horse shoe, in Spanish. It is called this because of the shape of the bay. When you drive down, from the coastal road, into La Herradura, the road down leads you directly to the sea front. Unfortunately, a few years ago, the local council there decided to re-design the sea front, using lots of old wooden railway sleepers. They made walkways running the length of the beach, and a sort of pier that juts out into the sea. The pier always reminds me of part of the Bridge on the River Kwai (in the film), in my mind, it was a monstrosity. The walkway took just a few short years since it was first installed, to deteriorated so badly, that it became dangerous and unusable. Fortunately, the local council have since removed most of it, and at the time of writing, are considering what to replace it with.

With or without its wooden folly, La Herradura is a beautiful place. It has a beauty which appeals to me. The great shape of the bay itself, and the wonderful views that you get from there, and all the chiringuitos and restaurants that stretch almost around the whole length of the bay. If you walk to the eastern end of the bay, you will find a very large chiringuito, called Chambeo de Joaquin, which is open throughout the year. Every Sunday, its owner, Joaquin, cooks an enormous paella, similar to what Ayo cooks in Nerja, but I must say, that Joaquin's paella, is the better of the two. Paella, by the way, is pronounced 'pae-aya,' the letters 'Ls' are pronounced like a 'Y.'

You can of course, eat many other dishes besides paella at Chambeo de Joaquin's, all equally delicious, but I do advise you to book a table if you want to sit right on the beach at the front of the restaurant on a Sunday, as it is so popular, and people come from all over to eat there. If you do manage to get a table at the front, you will probably be served by Sabina, who is Swedish, and has worked there for a number of years.

She can speak numerous languages fluently, including, English, Spanish, German, French, and of course, Swedish, and no matter what you want, or how busy she is, and believe me, she is usually very busy, she will always do her best to help you, and to remember your name.

Joaquin, is something of a local celebrity, and is involved in raising money for various charities, both in Spain and South America. Joaquin had a younger brother named Dani, who ran the diving school in La Heradura. The building that housed the school, is still there, just along the sea front from Chambeo de Joaquin's, but alas, poor Dani, is not. He was found one night, at the wheel of his car, very close to the diving school, shot dead. As far as I know, his death still remains a mystery.

Until a year or two ago, you could always watch the antics of para gliders, from the beach at La Heradura. They used to take off from a nearby high point, and perform various tricks and feats above your head, before finally coming down to land on the beach. You do still get the odd one or two, but the vast majority were stopped, apparently by the owners of the house on the hill, whose property they used to take off from, which was a shame for all us spectators, but not I suppose, if you were the owner of the house, and you had a regular procession of guys in rubber suits, along with all their paraphernalia, tramping all over your land every other day, and jumping off the cliff at the end of your garden.

Even though Dani's diving club no longer exists, snorkelling and diving are still as popular as ever here, as it is particularly clear water in this area, with lots of undersea life. There is a snorkelling club that operates from Nerja, and organises trips to La Herradura for this.

Just before you get to Chambeo de Joaquin's, along the sea front, there is another chiringuito, which I really love, called Rebalaja. You cannot miss this, as it is painted bright blue, and has beautiful flowering plants climbing all over the front. The food is much the same as in Chambeo de Joaquin's, except that they do not cook a giant paella, although you can still order paella from the menu if you want it. They do not cater as much for tourists as Joaquin's do, and seem to cater more for local people, with some wonderful game dishes, as well as the usual fish dishes. What I like most about Rebalaja's are their tapas, which are of course, free with your drinks. I also like to stand or sit, at the open air bar, and look through the palm trees at the wonderful view in front of you, and listen to the music from their CD player. This is usually something typically Spanish, but no matter what is playing, it always seems to add to the wonderful atmosphere there. A couple of years ago, the local police had a crackdown on loud music being played, and for some reason, unbeknown to me, decided to take Rebalaja's music system away from them, and close them down for a while. I couldn't believe this, as their music was never loud and certainly didn't intrude upon anyone that I knew of. When they did eventually open again, still without their music system, they played their music through a mobile phone and two tiny speakers, which I thought was really amusing, as this was the bar that had been shut down for supposedly loud music, and here they were playing music on a mobile phone. Thankfully, everything is back to normal again now, and you can still enjoy, the food, the drinks, the views, and the music, on a completely new music system.

Marina del Este

Back on the N340 again, and heading further eastwards, just 5 minutes past La Heradura, you come to the turn off towards Marina del Este. Don't get too worried that you might be heading in the wrong direction, as the road snakes upwards, higher and higher. The reason for this, is that they built all the houses and villas up on high ground above the marina, in order to give them the wonderful views that you will see as you drive up there. The road then slopes down again until you eventually reach Marina del Este, which is a yachting marina that was built quite recently. It is a lovely looking place, with a small beach, and a variety of designer type shops and waterside restaurants, offering great food, with wonderful views of the marina. If you have just won the lottery, or maybe just want to dream about what it would be like if you had, then grab yourself a quayside table at one of the restaurants, and pick out which yacht you would like, there are plenty there to choose from. Or if a yacht isn't quite your thing, maybe you might want to pick one of the villas up in the hills above you? Still worth the trip though, even if you only have a drink there, take in the scenery, and do a spot of day-dreaming.

Almuñécar

Ten minutes further eastwards past Marina del Este, brings you to Almuñécar. This is a large sprawling town, with a very strong Spanish feel about it. It has, up to now, escaped the mass tourist invasion, which other towns of this size along the coast have endured, and probably grown rich on. It has miles of wide sandy beaches, and a water park, which is open during the summer months. The beaches however, are marred only by the rather high apartment blocks that were built sometime in the 1960s. But I must say, that unattractive as these blocks look, they all face directly to the sea, and the views from them are simply out of this world.

This part of the coast is known as the Costa Tropical. This is for its sub tropical climate, and the amazing selection of plants, flowers and fruits that grow here. In the centre of the old part of the town, is Majuelo Park, which has one of the largest outside collections of tropical and subtropical plants in Europe. There are more than 400 exotic trees, bushes and other plants, from the fragrant frangipani to the majestic royal palm.

During the summer months, various fiestas and other events take place here in the park, such as a week long Jazz Festival, which, for one reason or another I always seem to miss. The festival that I don't miss however is the Feria Gastronómica (Gastronomic festival), which takes place in May. This is when all the local restaurants compete with each other by selling small portions of the various dishes they serve from small individual stands. There is also a bar set up nearby, so all you need to do is get yourself a beer or a glass of wine, find a table, if you can, and then start sampling the many dishes on offer, and believe me, there are plenty to choose from. Live music is provided by various artists, who perform on a small stage, which is a permanent feature in the park. As evening starts to fall, a real party atmosphere takes over, with non-stop music, dancing and singing. The nearby Castillo de San Miguel (Castle of Saint Michael), which towers over the park, is floodlit, and forms a perfect backdrop to this fiesta that goes on for three days. It is a truly magical setting.

The park also houses the remains of Roman salazones, or salting pits, where they used to used to preserve their fish in the salt. The fishing industry was very important during ancient times, and Sexi, as Almuñécar was then called by the Romans, was considered one of the most important fish-salting centres in the Mediterranean. Only a part of the original Roman complex has been excavated and further constructions still lie beneath the rest of the park, but the park has become so important to the locals, and visitors alike, that further work has been put off for the foreseeable future. There is a bridge that runs over the salt pits, which houses small workshops, used by local artisans. One of these is a guitar maker's workshop, where I heard the most wonderful classical Spanish guitar being played one day. During the day, the only sounds you normally hear in the park, are the sounds of the birds singing, or the Peacocks, from the nearby bird sanctuary, so when I heard this wonderful, sweet sound of the guitar, I went to investigate, and I saw the guitar maker, carrying on with his work within the shop, while a man, presumably a happy customer, sat on a chair in the doorway and played softly and superbly, a beautiful classical piece. When he finished I applauded him and walked away, with tears in my eyes.

The old part of the town is full of narrow, winding streets, some of which, lead up to the Castillo de San Miguel, which dominates Almuñécar's skyline. Originally built by the Romans in the 1st century BC, the Moors developed the castle into an impressive fortress whose defences included three separately walled precincts, 46 towers and turrets and three main gates. During the Middle Ages, particularly during latter reigns of the Nasrid kings in Granada, the castle was used by sultans as their beachside retreat and also as dungeons to house political prisoners.

In 1489, after 25 days of fighting, Moslem Almuñécar capitulated to Christian forces. It was the last town to fall before Granada, three years later. At this time the castle became known by its current name, after the new patron saint, San Miguel. Remodelling began under Charles V, during which time, the main entrance consisting of four towers, the drawbridge (now gone) and the moat, were all built. For the next 300 years the castle continued to guard the town against threats from Berber pirates.

Its final action was seen in 1810 during the War of Independence. At this time Almuñécar was occupied by Napoleon's troops and the fortifications were attacked from the sea by British warships causing enough damage to put the castle out of action. After the French left in 1814, it fell into disuse. In the early 1980s the castle precincts were cleared and excavations and restoration commenced.

It is now open every day for visitors except Mondays. But even when closed, the views from up there are outstanding. But be warned, the steep hike up there can be somewhat tiring if you are not a very keen walker.

If you do decide on a visit to the castle, you will almost certainly want to sit and relax for a while when you do get back down to flat ground once again, and there are several plazas filled with tables and chairs from the nearby cafes and bars where you can do this. Plaza de la Constitucion, where the town hall is, seems to be the favourite during the daytime, especially on Fridays, which is market days, when many visitors flock to Almuñécar.

Tapas really is a way of life in Almuñécar, and every bar and cafe compete strongly with each other, producing more and more delicious variations for you to try, all completely free of course, with every drink you purchase. I am constantly amazed, how the staff always know exactly how many drinks you have consumed, and what tapas you have had. They call out their tapas orders to the kitchen, Primero (first), Segundo (second), Tercero (third), so that you never get the same tapa twice. I suppose you might if you decided to stay for the whole evening, and wanted to eat non-stop. I have never done this, although I must admit I have come quite close to it on occasions.

A five-minute walk from here takes you to Plaza Kalibia, which is like no place I have ever seen before. It is lined all around the edges with open fronted bars with stools in front of them, and the whole of the centre of the square is packed with tables and chairs. During the day, you might find one or two of these bars open, with the occasional customer relaxing with their drink, but at night, you wouldn't believe it was the same place. It starts to fill up from about 9pm onwards, and by midnight, you have to be very lucky to find a stool or seat anywhere, and it doesn't stop at midnight either, it goes on into the early hours, until the last customer has gone. But, what I particularly like about Plaza Kalibia, is that it isn't just one age group that gathers there, as you would imagine with such a late place. You get all age groups there, from teenagers, to middle aged, to old age pensioners. You even see families with babies in prams, and young children, happily running around and playing, as it is a completely safe, and pedestrianised area, where no motor vehicles can drive through.

One problem that I can never get to the bottom of, is the speed of which the bars in Almuñécar, seem to change hands. You get to know the owner, and he gets to know you, and what you like to drink, and then you leave, only to find upon your return a month or two later, that a different owner has taken over.

There used to be a small bar called El Cid, in a side street next to the town hall. This was a lovely looking bar, with open brickwork and marble and lots of ironwork, and the tapas were second to none, but there was seldom anyone in there. I put this down to the owner, who was a miserable looking man, who always stood at the far end of the bar, reading a newspaper, never smiling or talking. He would just grunt at you when he gave you your drink, or tapas, and didn't even bother to say goodbye to you, when you left.

The next time I visited Almuñécar, I decided not to bother with this small bar, but to go straight to one of my favourite bars, called Bar Meson, in the Plaza de la Constitucion. I couldn't believe my eyes when I got inside, for there was the old misery from El Cid's bar around the corner, and he was now running this place. 'Oh God,' I thought, he will now ruin this place as well with his miserable ways, but on the contrary, he was a changed person, happy and smiling, and playing music on the CD player. He was even chatting up the girls in there. Over the next few weeks I got to know him, and to quite like him, but, a month or two later, he was gone again, and someone else was in charge.

The next time I visited Almuñécar, yet another change had taken place. This time there was a young guy in charge of Bar Meson, who seemed to model himself on Tom Cruise, in the movie, "Cocktail", with his exhibitions of bottle, glass, and ice juggling, which I must admit were quite impressive, although maybe not what one would expect in a typically Spanish bar in this part of the world. Needless to say, at the time of writing, the ownership of the bar has changed yet again. It now seems to be owned by a couple, who have made it a great success. Not exactly my cup of tea I am afraid, as he has concentrated more on attracting tourists to the outside area, and ignoring the inside bar completely. This constant change over doesn't just apply to the owners of the bars, it also applies to the customers as well.

When I first started going to Bar Meson, I met two English guys, who both lived locally, one of whom was married and the other, a bit of an old rocker, who lived on his own. They were nice guys, very friendly and very funny, and they were in there every night. They told me that they had both lived in Almuñécar for years, and how you could always find them propping the bar up in Bar Meson. I even used to see one of them always walking around the town during the day. I remember bumping into him one day in the town, and he told me how he had just been on the Internet, and had seen an Exercet Missile for sale. 'Can you believe it?' He said, 'they can nick you for drink driving, yet you can buy a bleeding Exercet Missile on the Internet, and that's legal?' He really made me laugh, and I took it for granted that both him and his friend would always be around, like a part of Almuñécar. But I am sorry to say that is not the case, for I haven't seen either of these two characters from that day to this. Not exactly a big deal I know, but just strange how one minute people are here, saying that they are part of the structure of the place, so to speak, and the next moment, they are gone, as if they never existed in the first place. Unless he bought the Exercet Missile of course, and blew himself and his friend up with it, who knows?

Getting back to the bar owners, I often wonder if they are on some sort of rota system, where they all have to take a turn of running a bad bar, followed by running a good one? One place that never changes, and is always good, is the Bar - Restaurant Avenida, in Avenida de Europa, which is the same street that the park is in. It is run by two partners, Lute and Jesus, and has both inside and outside dining areas. It serves wonderful food, huge portions, and at very cheap prices. The staff and owners are always friendly, and it is nearly always packed. So if you do want a table there, you might have to be prepared to wait. One of the first times that I ever went into Bar Avenida, I had a drink at the bar, and was given, as a tapa, a rather ugly looking fish, whose name I do not know, but it is always served in a sort of circle, where its tail is stuffed into its mouth. Actually, it tastes a lot better than what it looks. An old local man came in and stood next to me, and ordered a drink. When he got his drink, they gave him some fried aubergine as a tapa, and did this guy complain! He kept pointing at my fish, and telling them that is what he wanted, and why should he be given rubbishy vegetables when I was having fish? Lute just smiled, took away the aubergine and brought the old man a fish, the same as mine. Can you imagine that happening in the UK, you are given some free food and you complain that it isn't good enough for you and that you want something else instead? You would be told to take a running jump or something similar. But that is the difference between Spain and the UK, one of the many reasons why I love it so much.

Another bar/restaurant, right in the centre of town, is Francisco's. It is a large, and very old looking place, which looks like it hasn't been modernised or redecorated since it was originally opened, sometime in the 1940s or thereabouts. On one wall, is an enormous stuffed boar's head, with dust so thick on the top, that when I first saw it, I thought it was grey hair. The place is owned and run by Francisco, whom I would take a guess at being about 70 years old. He is a nice old man, always ready with a smile, but I must admit that I am not over keen on his tapas, or the look of the food they serve in there, and the only reason I ever went in there, was for the curiosity value, as it makes you feel as if you have travelled back in time somewhat.

When I next walked past there, my wife asked me if I wasn't going to go in there, and when I said no, she replied that she felt sorry for him, as he was just a poor old man, trying to eke out a living in a bar that had probably been handed down to him from his father, or even his grandfather. She made me feel so bad that we did go in there again, and never went past without having just one drink in there.

A little while later, I found another restaurant, called Francisco 11, which I never associated at all with Francisco's, as this one was very upmarket, with a small terrace outside, and very good waiter service. It wasn't until my wife and I had been in this restaurant several times, and had got to know the owner, that we found out that he was the grandson of old Francisco, and that old Francisco owned both buildings. So this poor old man who had won my wife's sympathy, was in fact, not far short of being a millionaire property owner!

A bar which is something of a mystery to me, is the Máscara Bar, which was, or is, in Plaza de la Victoria. It is quite small inside, but also has outside seating. I have used this bar, on and off for at least 4 years. The atmosphere is good, and the drinks and tapas, excellent. But, now comes the mystery. When I called in there last, the first thing I noticed, was the name outside had been changed from the Máscara Bar, to "Caza Mayor Tu Taberna". The man, whose name I never knew, but assumed to be the owner of the place, was not there any more (nothing unusual in that in Almuñécar), but there was a woman behind the bar whom I had seen in there before. I asked her what had happened to the owner, and she told me that he had bought a car wash, of all things, and was now running that. So why did she change the name, I asked her? She looked at me quizzically, and shook her head, stating that the name had not been changed. 'But it was the Máscara Bar before' I said. 'No' she replied, 'it has always been Caza Mayor'. I didn't want to argue with her, after all, it was her place now, (I think). Who knows? After all, this is Almuñécar!

A few steps up a very steep and narrow alley from the main street, that leads up to the castle, is probably one of the strangest and authentic bars in Almuñécar. It is called Los Pajaritos and is run by one man behind the bar, and his wife and daughter in the kitchen. It is quite small, with a few tables and chairs to one side and a bar the other side. I think the owner's name is Pepe, a rather large man with a permanent three-day growth of beard, who I am informed is a fisherman during the day. The toilet facilities in Los Pajaritos consist of two narrow metal doors that lead directly into basic toilet areas; no sinks or anything else, just the basic toilets.

It is not the toilets however, that customers go into Los Pajaritos for, it is the extremely cheap drinks and the enormous tapas that his wife and daughter cook up from the tiny kitchen to one side of the bar. From the main street, you would be hard pressed to know there was even a bar there, although there is an old sign still hanging outside, but it isn't until you walk up the slope and get to the actual door that the noise hits you. It seems that everyone in Almuñécar must be in there, and all shouting at the same time.

If you do manage to make it there, I would advise having the beer, that is if you do not mind drinking directly from the bottle. At least the beer comes from the fridge and is cold. When I went there with my wife, she ordered a glass of rosado, which Pepe poured from a misted up vase type thing, which looked like a specimen jar. Not only did it look awful, it wasn't even cold! But to think we got a plate of 8 giant prawns free of charge with the two drinks, we decided against complaining.

On what was probably my first visit to Almuñécar, I discovered a hidden gem of a bar, called Meson Muralla. Like most places, it was both a bar and a restaurant but to find it wasn't exactly the easiest of jobs, in fact I first found it purely by accident, while wandering the many little back streets and alleys there. Through an archway from the main square, down some steps, following the narrow little alleys, and down another flight of steps, and I was suddenly stopped in my tracks by a cacophony of noise, growing ever louder as we grew nearer. Meson Muralla sat down a cul-de-sac, which it also used as an outside seating area. The noise of course, was nothing more than people chatting, or maybe some shouting, as the Spanish as a whole, are known to be quite a noisy race. Inside it was almost impossible to get to the bar, but when you did, and collected your tapa and found somewhere to stand, it was worth it. The place just buzzed with excitement, and the clientele was composed of mainly affluent looking Granadians, many of whom tend to use Almuñécar as their weekend bolt-hole. I had one problem with this place, and that was that I had found it on my last night, for the next day I was heading back to Britain. I made a mental note of the address, which was Calle Angel Gomez, which is close to Plaza Noreta.

Upon my next visit, there was no need to ask where I would head for first, and much to my surprise, Meson Muralla was still there, but with an addition to its name; it was now Meson Muralla de Flores, and as you might have guessed, the management had changed. The food in the restaurant was still as good, but the exciting buzz had gone.

There was also a new girl behind the bar, very attractive, somewhat Arabic in appearance. She was very friendly, always smiling and practising her English on me. As Mason Muralla is usually my last stopping off place before making my way home, you can take it as a pretty safe bet, that by the time I get there, I have usually had slightly more than one or two drinks! But, when I looked the following morning at the bill which the Arabic girl had given me, and I had paid, for just four glasses of wine, which was two for Frances and two for myself), plus a few stuffed mussels, I found that she had charged me 40 Euros.

I did of course, question her on this, and after some time, with her working frantically on a piece of paper, she returned to tell me that I had drunk more than that, and had more to eat than what I said. I knew that I hadn't of course, because even though we did arrive late that evening, we had not exactly been drinking excessively, but trying to put that argument across 24 hours after the event, is pretty pointless, and got me nowhere. I decided there and then, that I would watch and count exactly what we had in the future, so that I could put my point across there and then if it happened again.

I could hardly believe my ears, when it did happen again, just a couple of nights later. This time the bill was correct, but my change was ten Euros short. Luckily for me I noticed it straight away this time, and she quickly gave me the ten Euros. Were these two incidents both accidental? I would like to think so, as I have never experienced anything like this before anywhere in Spain, and this particular girl seemed so nice.

Needless to say, I started not frequenting Mason Muralla so much after that, and it seemed that many other people did the same, as the last time I visited it was almost empty. Whether it was the change of management, or the girl behind the bar I don't know, but Mason Muralla closed soon after that, and has never been opened again by anyone else since.

As you will no doubt appreciate, Almuñécar has many bars and restaurants, even though they close and open on a seemingly never-ending carrousel. One bar which is consistent, and has been there ever since my first visit, is Meson Gala, which is in a pretty little square, with a small park opposite, called Plaza Gala.

Meson Gala is an old fashioned bar with plenty of woodwork and small windows that open up, to the street, where there are stools and barrels to sit around. Since the demise of Mason Muralla, Meson Gala seems to have taken over with the Granadian crowd.

As I was sitting outside Meson Gala one night I heard a lot of noise and chatting coming from somewhere nearby. Just across the street in Calle Granada, I noticed a large crowd of people outside what looked like a new bar. This was like the preverbal red flag to the bull. Within a couple of minutes I had dragged my wife over there, ordered a drink and found a place to sit under the outside awning. This was indeed a new place, called Entre Vino and like Mason Muralla before it, it was buzzing!

Considering there must have been approximately fifty to seventy people there, there was only one person serving behind the bar, and one girl serving outside where I was, and between them they handles it perfectly, and with a smile. At this particular time, the smoking-ban had just been enforced in Spain, meaning that if you want to smoke, you should do it outside. As I said there were quite a lot of people inside, and being a very hot night as well, meant that the windows were open wide. One woman in there was perched on the edge of the window-ledge, chatting away to her friends and happily smoking at the same time. She held her cigarette just out the window, and no one took the slightest notice. Can you imagine that same scene happening in the UK? The police would have been called, the woman forcibly ejected, and probably fined into the bargain. But this is Spain, where the average citizen has a much more relaxed attitude to life than we do in the UK.

I love people like her, and went up to her and congratulated her on her courage. She didn't quite understand what I meant, as according to her, this was the Spanish way of life, and no one was going to make her change it.

I always get a little sad every time I drive out of Almuñécar, it's like leaving an old friend or a lover. Will they still be there when you next return, and if they are, how much will they have changed? Up until now, Almuñécar hasn't changed too much from when I first discovered it, and I certainly hope that it stays that way.

Frigiliana

Back on the N340 once again, you can either turn right, and head in the direction of Granada, or you can turn left, and head back towards Nerja. To get to Granada from Almuñécar, once you pick up the motorway, it will only take you about 50 minutes. You don't have to use the motorway of course, you can take the old road to Granada, up through the mountains and across country. I did this once from the village of Competa, taking all the old roads, through mountain passes and gorges, and across miles of flat open plains, finally reaching Granada about 4 hours later. A long drive maybe, but what marvellous countryside, and views. It was an experience more than a drive. If you have plenty of time and love the country as I do, then try it, you won't regret it, but if it is during the summer, remember to take plenty of water to drink, you're going to need it!

I won't attempt here to describe the city of Granada, as it probably warrants a book of its own. Most visitors go there to see the famous and beautiful, Alhambra, but there is so much more to see and do in Granada, and the best way, is to take a trip there, stay at least a night or two, and explore it for yourself.

Back on the N340 again, and heading west towards the direction of Nerja, there are a number of other villages and towns, worth visiting. You can of course, pick up the motorway, and get to most of these places in less time than the old N340 coastal road, but I am sure you won't find it as interesting, plus of course, when you are driving on this road, you can stop off at any time you feel like it. You can pull right onto the beach if you like, and have a little swim in between your drive, or stop just to take some photos or have something to eat or drink. You can't do any of these things on the big, wide, Autovia (motorway).

When you reach the main Nerja roundabout, if you turn right, instead of turning left into Nerja town, this road takes you to Frigiliana. It is only 7 kilometres up the gentle hills and bends before you reach the typical pueblo blanco (white village) of Frigiliana that sits reasonably high on a mountain ridge overlooking the sea with spectacular panoramic views.

Frigiliana is important from an historical viewpoint. El Fuerte, the hill that sits above the village, was the scene of the final bloody defeat of the Moors of La Axarquía in their 1569 rebellion. On the top of the hill, lies the remains of a ruined fort from which some of the Moors reputedly threw themselves, rather than be killed or captured by the Spanish. Legend has it, that bones and rusted weapons dating from this battle still lie among the scrub on El Fuerte.

Frigiliana was voted the prettiest village in Andalucía by the Spanish tourism authority; the village is a web of narrow cobbled streets lined with whitewashed houses, with wrought iron balconies filled with planters of brilliant red geraniums. Small plazas provide shady seating, and some excellent outdoor restaurants, while the village bars are popular with visitors who come here to taste the locally produced wine. There are also many excellent shops selling pottery and ceramics, including decorative plates with their distinctive Arab design.

I wouldn't advise driving your car into the village itself, as many of its streets are very narrow and winding, and trying to find a parking space can be quite difficult. Personally, I always leave my car at the car park at the bottom of the hill and walk up into the village itself. Frigiliana is best explored on foot, but be aware, that its streets are often very steep, so be prepared for the occasional stop at one or other of the local bars, in order to get your breath back (that's my excuse anyway). There is also a regular bus service that runs from Nerja, or alternatively, coach tour trips are also organised from there.

Torrox

Next stop along the coastal road is Torrox, which is split into two parts, Torrox Costa (Torrox coast) and Torrox Pueblo (Torrox village). Torrox is sheltered from the Northern winds by the Sierras Tejeda (Tejeda mountains). The pueblo is still largely untouched by tourist development, and you can truly appreciate the Spanish way of life here, with its narrow winding streets, and both mountain and sea views. Torrox has its own Moorish Quarter and wine and raisin presses and a Sugar Factory, which has very interesting industrial architecture. The nearby mountains also house a National Hunting Reserve.

Torrox has a busy festive calendar all the year round, its most important festival being from October 4th and 8th. The Fiesta de las Migas takes place on the last Sunday before Christmas, a festival in which visitors to the town can sample this exquisite dish accompanied by a glass of wine from the area and music and dancing in the streets.

The actual word Migas, means breadcrumbs, but leave it to the frugal Spaniards to elevate a simple dish of stale breadcrumbs into the world of gastronomic delights. Migas, is so beloved throughout much of Spain, and Torrox in particular, that this annual Fiesta de Migas takes place, drawing tens of thousands of people.

At its most basic, migas consists of leftover bread torn into small bits, slightly moistened with water, and then fried in olive oil with garlic and pimentón, (Spanish paprika). Every region seems to have its own variation on the theme, most of which call for the cook to add healthy doses of cured pork products, such as chorizo (dry-cured paprika-laced sausage), morcilla (blood sausage), jamón serrano, and bacon. The dish also often includes peppers and onions in the mix and, surprisingly, may be garnished with a handful of green grapes. It can also be topped with various other humble delicacies, including sardines.

Torrox Costa, is only some 4 kilometres from Torrox Pueblo. It has beautiful beaches, promenades, restaurants, shops, night life, tennis courts, swimming pools, in fact everything for the tourist. There are also ruins of a Roman Village at the Torrox Lighthouse, which is protected as a Property of Cultural Interest. It is this combination of old and new that makes Torrox such an interesting place to stay. Here you can have a quiet villa holiday in the Torrox countryside with the convenience of easy access to modern Costa del Sol holiday resort facilities.

In between Torrox and Torre del Mar, which is the next big town along the coast, are the tiny hamlets of Mezquitilla and Lagos, both still basically, fishing villages, but, I am sorry to say, with more and more new villas and apartments being erected all the time. You can count the actual fisherman's cottages that are left along the main road now, on the fingers of one hand.

Algarrobo

Just before you get into Torre del Mar, you come to Algarrobo, which, like Torrox, is split into two parts, Algarrobo Pueblo, and Algarrobo Costa. The Pueblo is very nice, and retains a Moorish quality about it. The Rio Algarrobo flows gently through the village where horses are often found grazing on the banks. The parish church of Santa Ana dates from 1505 although the current building was built in the 17th century. There is also a large, attractive, tropical park in the village next to a large communal village swimming pool and tennis courts.

Algarrobo Costa, once a fishing village, is now mostly dedicated to tourism with high-rise apartment blocks along the sandy beach. A few years ago, I used to use one of these beaches, not because it was particularly beautiful, because it wasn't. What I liked about it, was the fact that you didn't get too many people there, like you can do on the more popular beaches, you could choose an isolated spot and could more or less guarantee that it would stay that way for the rest of the day. There was also, a lovely little chiringuito called Noni's, built right on the beach and surrounded by banana palms. They cooked good simple food there and played good music, never too loudly, just right to set a good atmosphere. This particular chiringuito was made from bamboo, with a palm leaf roof, which meant that it could not be locked up at night, so the barman, who was a young guy named Jose, had to sleep on a made up bed behind the bar. It was really funny if you got there early in the morning before Jose was up yet. You would see the bamboo blinds roll back and a weary looking Jose peak out to see if the sun was up yet. He would shower with cold water, using a hose in one of the nearby portaloos. My wife and I spent many happy hours on that beach and at Noni's chiringuito, and then came the inevitable day, when Frances and I returned, after being away for a few months to find Noni's had been demolished.

The local council has since built a sort of raised platform where Noni's used to stand, with a statue on it, for what reason I don't know, it certainly wasn't to commemorate Noni's. They haven't allowed for another chiringuito to open up close by to take Noni's place, and they also closed down a family run, sun bed business, so without somewhere to eat or drink, and no sunbeds to lie on, I personally think they have ruined a really nice, simple little beach area.

Back onto the N340 coastal road again, and you will notice that it is dotted with watchtowers built in the 16th century for defence over the beaches. There are two of these at Algarrobo, the Torre Ladeado and the Torre Derecha and another at the small coastal village of Lagos.

Torre del Mar

Finally, we come to Torre del Mar, where there are wide sandy beaches flanked by a long beachfront promenade with wonderful views along the coast and of the hills and mountains behind, dotted with white houses and villages. From the beach here, I always look across the vast bay in the direction of Rincón de la Victoria, where you can see, on a clear day, the huge cut out bull advert for Osborne Brandy, which stands proudly on a hilltop, which to me, and I am sure thousands of other people, represents not just an advert for a drinks company, but an advert for Spain itself.

The scenery along this part of the coast, is quite wide and spectacular, and trips can be arranged to spot dolphins and other marine life, from a motor launch run by the Caleta Cruise Club, which operates from La Caleta de Velez, which is just two kilometres away to the east. There is also a fishing port and yachting marina at La Caleta de Velez. This area has not yet been developed as a tourist attraction but remains very much a working port. There is just one bar/restaurant that overlooks the marina itself, although there is a choice of several to the right of the port entrance.

Torre del Mar is not exactly beautiful, in the traditional sense, but it has so much character and real Spanish atmosphere. The vast beach is extremely well kept, as is the Paseo Maritimo de Poniente, which is the wide promenade that runs alongside it. There are many chirrguitos all along the promenade, serving local delicacies all day during the summer months, including Sardinas al Espeto (Sardines on a Spit), which are fresh sardines hot and crusty from the espeto, which is a split and sharpened piece of bamboo cane passed through several sardines to serve as a skewer. This is usually cooked right on the beach itself.

Old fishing boats, filled with sand, are used for this, where a fire is lit in the mound of sand inside the boat, and then burned down to its embers. The espetos are set in the sand at an angle to the fire so that the sardines cook in the heat but not the smoke, and they are turned half way through. The sardines have been previously covered in coarse sea salt but neither gutted nor cleaned. This is probably one of the cheapest meals you can have in Spain, but to sit outside at a chiringuito, facing the sea, having just watched your lunch being cooked on the beach in front of you, takes some beating. No messing around with knives and forks, all you need are your fingers to eat these little delicacies, and follow up by washing them down with a nice cold beer, or glass of wine. And all for about 6 Euros, where else could you do this?

If you leave the beach and walk towards the main road, the Avenida de Andalucia, which is really a continuation of the N340, you should try to walk through the Paseo de Larios, which is a beautiful park, which leads up to the Inglesia Andres Aposal (Church of Andrew the Apostle). You could be forgiven for thinking that this park had been there for years, but in fact, the park as you see it now, with its lush vegetation, flowers, palms, and water fountains, has only just been completed in the last few years, about 2003. I remember when I first saw work being started to uproot the old park, I was devastated, how could they do this to such a lovely park, I thought. But now, when I walk through the new park as it is today, I realise what an improvement they have made to it, how much lighter it is, and as the sides are now pedestrianised as well, how much more people friendly it has become.

The Avenida de Andalucia, is filled with shops, restaurants, bars, cafes, and as usual, estate agents, and being a main road, is always busy. If you are looking for a bargain, then this is the area to shop at. I am talking mainly about clothes and shoes, which I have found here at least 30 to

50 per cent cheaper than along the coast, but in general, most things are somewhat cheaper here, probably because it is a mainly Spanish area.

But Torre del Mar is not just about beaches and shopping for bargains. It is also a place where young people flock to, especially in the summer time, to gather at a 500 metre stretch along the seafront, called El Copo, which is a continual line of bars and discotheques that are open from around 10pm until 6am every morning in the summer and at weekends during the winter. But there is no need to worry, if this isn't exactly what you are looking for. This is a relatively small area, and Torre del Mar is a big place, and I am sure you will find peace and tranquility, if that is what you are looking for, in another part of the town, away from El Copo.

My personal favourite during the day, is the area between the main road and the sea front, where you will find untold numbers of Marisquerias (sea food bars/restauarants). These are big, and very modern looking places, usually with tiled or marble walls, and stainless steel bars, with cold cabinets where you will see the most amazing displays of fresh fish and shellfish you could ever wish for. Seating is usually at the stools provided along the length of the bar, and sometimes, a few others placed here and there, according to how much room there is. There are also seating areas with normal tables and chairs outside, but these areas are usually for customers who want to eat a proper meal, whereas the interior is specifically for drinks, with free tapas.

I don't know how many marisquerias there are in Torre del Mar, there must be dozens of them, if not more, but my personal favourite, and it would seem, half the town's as well, is one called El Yate (The Yacht) which is in a street just off the park, and close to the sea front. I nearly always drink beer in here, which is served from the tap, in little glasses, which I think hold about a third of a pint, and cost one Euro. If you want to order draught beer in Spain, you should ask for una caña (one drought), pronounced (oona can-ya). With every drink you buy, as in other tapas bars, you are given a free tapa, but here it is all seafood and shellfish, with the exception, now and again of some vegetables, such as Pimientos, or fried aubergine (berenjenas) pronounced (beren-hen-as).

I have been going to El Yate for quite a number of years, and I still see different dishes coming out of their kitchen almost every time I am there. But I find the atmosphere there, almost as good as the food, with local businessmen and bankers, standing beside local fisherman and farmers, and eating the same food. And as it starts to fill up, usually from 1pm onwards, the noise level increases so much that you literally have to shout to make yourself heard. When I first started going there, it was run then by a manager named Paco, who used to contribute greatly to the sound levels there, and he also spoke so quickly, it was like a machine gun being fired, which made it practically impossible for me to understand half of what he was saying. Paco left about a couple of years ago, and was replaced by a new manager, who, although his name is not Paco, still responds to this name. He shouts equally as loud as the old Paco, and is gradually developing the speed at which he shouts also. It took a while for the new Paco to get to know me, but as soon as he did, he absolutely inundated me with dish after dish of various free tapas, which is great, but can sometimes be rather funny, as he is a very short man, barely able to look over the top of the counter, so all you sometimes see, is a hand come up, and a dish slammed down onto the counter in front of you. Plates and glasses are never put onto the metal counter; they are banged onto it with great bravado, as if daring them to get broken. In a place where there can be up to a hundred people at times, no money ever changes hands until you have finished and are ready to leave. You are then asked what you had, how many drinks, and if you ordered anything else, which you might have to pay for. Everything is done on trust; can you imagine that happening in a British pub or bar?

The first Paco, who ran El Yate, now has his own place called Rincon El Paco, which is in a side street almost opposite El Yate. What I tend to do now, is have a few beers and tapas in Paco's, and follow that up by a nice relaxed lunch on the outside terrace of El Yate.

I have said before, that if you do know a little Spanish, you should try to use it as much as possible, but you should be prepared for a few knock backs maybe, as the Spanish spoken along this part of the coast, differs a great deal from that in other parts of Spain. Cuttlefish, for instance, is called Jibia, here, pronounced (hiby-ah), but when I went to Madrid once, and asked for Jibia, the waiter looked at me as if I was talking Russian or something. When I finally spotted it in his cooler cabinet, and pointed it out to him, he replied, 'ah sepia.' I told him that in Andalucia it was always called Jibia, to which he waved his hand dismissively in the air and said, 'Andalucia..hmmp'. I am not sure whether there is a little snobbery involved here, or do they genuinely not understand?

If you do decide to go to Torre del Mar and you do like fish, then you must try El Yate, but if you want to sit at the bar, then make sure that you get there early, or better still, try Paco's.

To me, Torre del Mar and seafood are inseparable, they go together like fish and chips, and if you look back at Torre's past, you can understand why. The origins of Torre del Mar goes back to at least the Phoenicians. Sites discovered include an 8th century BC 'Town of Toscanos' where there are remains of fish factories, a port and several houses, and a necropolis at Jardín. Torre del Mar takes its name, which translates to Tower of the Sea, from the many watch towers that used to guard the coast in Roman and Moorish times. I hope that they keep on guarding it from the tourist invasions that hit other towns to the west of here.

Competa

From Torre del Mar, we now start heading back eastwards once again, towards the direction of Nerja, but before we reach there, I would like to take one last detour, up to the village of Competa, which I have mentioned very briefly before. The best way to reach Competa, from the N340 coastal road, is to get to Torrox and then take the road inland, from there, which is sign posted, and takes you directly up to Competa.

Competa lies at an altitude of 636 metres, in the foothills of the Sierra Almijara. The drive up there takes about 40 minutes, and is narrow, winding, mountain roads all the way, so great care should be taken when attempting this drive, especially when doing it for the first time. The views are absolutely spectacular, but I do advise you not to try to take these in whilst still driving, just pull over into one of the places earmarked for stops such as this.

The area is irrigated by numerous springs and streams from the surrounding mountains. The nearby Casa de la Mira Nature Reserve is spectacularly beautiful, where all types of wildlife can be seen. The area produces avocados and other fruits and vegetables, but the main produce is the grape, from which the now quite famous wines of Competa are produced. Competa wine is known throughout Spain as a sweet wine, but they do also produce a dry variety, which is less well known.

On the 15th August every year, there is a popular Fiesta to celebrate Noche del Vino, (Night of the Wine), where flamenco and other music and dance accompany the free flowing wine. The Noche del Vino is a very old traditional party that has been celebrated for a long time. Traditionally the inhabitants of Competa went to their cortijos (farmhouses) up in the mountains during the vintage and didn't return until October, when the raisins were packed and the grapes had been pressed. On August the 15th they met at Plaza Almijara for a farewell party, where they sang and danced and drank the famous local wine.

Being highly significant for the people of Competa, the party was made official in 1975, and is now organised by the local council and includes a programme by which visitors can also get in touch with the local traditions.

During the morning of August 15th, there is demonstration of 'la pisa de la uva' (treading on grapes). There follows a free country style lunch with 'migas de harina' (garlic and meat cooked with bread crumbs), sardines, rural salad (peppers, oranges, onions, olives and tomatoes) and chorizo sausages. Both the pisa and the lunch are accompanied by local musicians. The party continues into the early hours of the next morning with music and dancing around the Plaza Almijara, which is still the main square, and houses the magnificent parish church of La Asunción, which was built in the 16th century in Baroque Mudejar style.

Competa is still a pretty village that has retained its original Moorish layout and has lots of interesting narrow streets and alleyways, with names such as Calle Laberinto, which literally means Labyrinth Street, but Competa is also, still very much a working village, in other words, not just turned over to tourism, although it does of course, cater for the tourist.

At the centre of Competa, lies the main square, the Plaza Almijara, which is dominated by the church on one side, and Perico's bar and restaurant, with its tables and chairs sprawling out everywhere, and usually filled with both visitors and locals alike, who like to sit, eat, drink and talk, and watch the world go by. From the plaza there is also a slope leading down beside the church to a much smaller square with another restaurant, whilst next to Perico's is yet another slope, which leads upwards, towards the top of the village, where my very good friend, Paco, whom I have mentioned earlier, has his excellent restaurant, Cortijo Paco.

When I first visited Competa, many years ago, Perico's in the main square, was probably one of the first places I went to. Although most visitors tend to sit outside, I always like to try the inside first, to sit up at the bar. I find that is the way that you meet and get talking to people, and find out what is happening and going on. One night, in Perico's, I overheard a very strange Spanish accent, and turned to see an elderly man along the bar, holding a very stilted conversation with the barman. I soon realised that the man was British, and was speaking a reasonable form of Spanish, but with a sort of Geordie accent, which, even when he spoke English, I found it quite difficult to understand. I got talking to him and found out that his name was Neil, he was about 79 years old, in quite frail health, and lived alone, in one of the houses just off the square.

Over the years, and many visits to Competa, I got to know old Neil quite well, as well as his little coterie of friends, one of whom, Pierre, who originally came from Guernsey, but who also now lived in Competa, with his wife, out on the campo. There were of course, other people in there, whom Neil knew, mostly Spanish, one was Jesus, who was about 45 years old, never been married and still living at home with his parents, he worked as a labourer on the land, didn't drink any alcohol at all, but could be really good company. Another was Enrique, who was, so Neil constantly told me, a master builder, 'if you want any building work or carpentry done, then you won't find better than Enrique' Neil would say.

Enrique made me laugh one day, when he was describing someone, and told me 'he is blind you know', but he pronounced the word "blind", to rhyme with "sinned", and for a moment I just could not work out what he was talking about. I suppose this is a really easy mistake to make when you are learning a language, especially one as complicated as English with so many pronunciations of a word, which is spelt the same way. I really used to look forward to Tuesday nights, when we would all meet up in Perico's

As old and as frail as Neil was, he still liked a good drink, and he was forever trying to chat up the ladies. When Jesus suggested one night that maybe we should all go down to the coast, to a disco, Neil was all for it, although I must say that I wasn't. Firstly, discos are not exactly my sort of thing, secondly, I wouldn't even contemplate driving down to the coast and then back up again, on those winding, sometimes treacherous roads, at night, without having had a drink, let alone after I had finished off more than a few in Perico's. And thirdly, even though I am not exactly a spring chicken myself, I cannot imagine turning up at a disco with a 79 year old man with a glass eye, and trying to act as if we were some cool dudes just blown into town, forget about it!

As I have already said, Jesus lived at home with his parents, and was a very nice man, but as far as I know, he had never had a girlfriend, although it wasn't for the lack of trying, but for some reason, old Neil, seemed to have better luck with the ladies than Jesus did. When I say better luck, I do not mean that literally. The women who walked into the bar at Perico's, usually did so for one reason only, and that was to use the washroom, and as Neil would be perched on his usual stool, just level with the toilets, he more of less had the pick of every lady that came in, but it was, as far as I ever saw, just friendly chat, and interest value as far as the ladies were concerned, I am sure. Jesus, on the other hand, just did not know what to say where women were concerned, and I did feel sorry for him.

When the annual Feria took place one year, Jesus informed everyone that he would be riding with the horsemen of the village. This takes place in the square, and was the prelude to the start of the Feria. Everyone gathered in the square and waited until the procession of horsemen started, approaching from a cobbled street opposite Perico's. Each horseman had a pretty senorita, riding side-saddle on the back of his horse, just behind him. When they got to the centre of the square, they would then show off their horsemanship, where the horse would usually rise up on its hind legs and do a sort of pirouette, or another move, which almost resembled tap dancing. Quite an impressive sight altogether.

The sight which I, and quite a few other were waiting to see, was of course, Jesus, would he really be taking part, and if so, how good would he be? Suddenly he appeared, his wonderful chestnut horse, clip clopping down the narrow, cobbled street opposite, and then entering the arena of the square. I must say that I was very impressed; he looked very good, in a grey waistcoat, a red bandana around his neck, and the usual wide, flat brimmed hat, like a Picador's castoreño, but in black instead of grey. He rode very well, and made his horse perform as good, if not better, than many of the other riders. The one thing that sadly let Jesus down, was as we had all suspected, the senorita on the back of his horse. She was pretty enough, and she was dressed beautifully, but, unlike all the other riders, whose senoritas were between the ages of 18 to 30, Jesus' senorita was just 10 years old, his niece, as she was the only girl who would agree to ride with him.

Naturally, I did congratulate him afterwards, but I also felt very sorry for him, and wondered what would eventually become of him after his parents died, and he was left on his own. Old Neil soon put me straight on that one, 'don't you go worrying yourself about him', he said, 'his family own so much property in Competa that when they do eventually die, Jesus will be a very rich man indeed'. That did make me feel somewhat better, but then money isn't everything, is it?

One Tuesday I walked in Perico's to find none of the usual crowd there. The barman told me that Neil wasn't well, and hadn't been out of his house for the last two weeks. I must admit that I was a little worried, and asked if anyone was looking after him, and how was he getting his food etc. The barman told me that a woman neighbour, who lived opposite Neil, and whom he always referred to as Mrs Nosey Parker, was looking in on him every day, and doing his washing and cleaning for him, whilst Perico's were sending in, completely free of charge, his twice daily meals. Can you imagine this happening in Britain? I certainly can't, not in London anyway, where I come from.

Not long after this, I am sorry to say, that Neil's health grew steadily worse, and the last I heard, he had been moved to a nursing home down on the coast somewhere near Malaga.

Competa, meanwhile, carries on with business (and pleasure) as usual. While El Noche del Vino seems to be enjoyed by everyone, local and visitors alike, I cannot say the same for the annual Ferria (fair). Although it does start off very good, with various attractions all around the village, including the show of horsemen, which I have just mentioned, and live music, drinking and dancing, in the communal swimming pool grounds, it gradually dissipates, until all that is left, are a few funfair rides in the car park at the bottom of the village. Nothing wrong with that you might think, but the time that I was staying there which coincided with the Ferria, the apartment I was staying at was at the top of the village, but directly overlooking the car park, and when you are trying to get to sleep, and the very loud music plays incessantly until the last person goes home, which was, when I was there, about six in the morning, I can assure you it is no fun, in fact it was so loud, that it actually made ants start coming out of the woodwork in the house. I put up with it, on that first night because I had no choice, but when I learned that it was going to go on for at least another night or two, that is when I decided to drive from there, across country, to Granada, as I have already spoken about earlier.

But please don't let me put anyone off going to Competa because of this. If you are not that keen on lots of loud noise and funfairs, then find out when the Feria is taking place, and simply make sure that your apartment or property does not overlook it, as mine did.

For a small village, there always seems to be something happening, more sometimes, than what you would usually find in the bigger resorts on the coast. As well as the usual restaurants, bars and cafes, there is also a couple of "clubs", but don't expect clubs, as in nightclubs, these are more like what we in Britain, would call working men's clubs. There is also, a "disco", where the local young people go, but by the look of what I have seen through the open doorway, it looks more like a church hall affair. But the "club", which I have been in several times, is called La Roca, and can be really good fun. There was a football match on between Real Madrid and another Spanish, team which I cannot remember the name of, and I was having a drink at the time, at a little bar called Laurie's Bar, pronounced (Layor-rie's), which is at the bottom of the village, by the car park. Laurie's team won, and I have never seen anyone move so quickly. He switched off the TV, started throwing all the plastic chairs from outside, into the bar area, and shouted 'everyone up to La Roca.' He locked the doors and was gone before I had hardly finished my drink.

I followed, along with everyone else, and got to La Roca as the party was about to begin. The dart-boards were closed away for the night, the pool tables covered up, and the local band started to tune up. People poured in, and within fifteen minutes the place was packed. Laurie was delirious at his team winning, and was buying drinks for everyone, including my wife and myself, so naturally, when his wife came in, I offered to buy her a drink, and asked her what she would like. 'I would like a bie-lis', she told me. I asked again, and got the same answer, so, never having heard of this drink, I went to the bar, and did my best to pronounce this unknown drink to the barman, exactly as she had pronounced it, thinking that if it was some local drink, he would most probably know it. I was quite shocked when he didn't question me at all, and just turned around and poured out a glass of Baileys. They say that you learn something new every day, I certainly did that day. But this is what I love about Spain, the friendliness and warmth of the people, everyone mixes, and it doesn't matter if they have only known you a relatively short time, you are still invited and accepted into their society. I think we in Britain could learn a lot from this culture.

The first time I encountered this type of thing in Competa, was in a restaurant, not far from the main square, called El Pilón. At this time it was owned by my friend Paco, who now owns Cortijo Paco. I hadn't known Paco long, and was just about to leave one night, after a thoroughly enjoyable meal, when Paco came into the room my wife and I were in, and invited us to stay, for some sort of party. My knowledge of Spanish at that time was not very good, not that it is marvellous now, and I just about understood that it was a birthday party they were celebrating.

All of the staff were there, along with Paco and his wife and their very young son, Paco Junior, as well as some other people, whom I assumed were all part of his family and friends. We were all invited out onto one of the terrace areas, where a large table had been set up, along with free tapas and drinks. An elderly man, who somewhat resembled Paco, was the obvious guest of honour, and was presented with a large home made birthday cake, with which he attempted to blow out all the candles. It was a great night, where, I am sorry to say, I consumed a lot more wine than I had intended to, but Frances, (my wife), had her camera with her, and took a number of photos of the event, probably to show me later, to prove how drunk I had been.

Funnily enough, when the pictures were developed, as they used to be in those days, before digital cameras, I didn't look at all drunk, but she did manage to get some very good shots of Paco, with his arm around his father, as he blew out the candles. I had some extra copies made of these, and gave them to Paco, as I thought he might like them, especially the ones with his father. Paco couldn't stop laughing when I gave them to him, and he explained to me, in his best English, which was far better than my Spanish, that this man wasn't his father at all, he was just a local man who used to help Paco, by tending the outdoor barbecue, on which various dishes were cooked.

Again, what I am trying to point out here is the genuine warmth of the Spanish people. He had held a special birthday party for this man, who was after all, just a casual worker, he had baked him a cake and invited all these people, and supplied food and drink for everyone. You might hear about pop stars and film stars doing this sort of thing for people in Britain, but I can't recall ever hearing about a normal working man doing it, which Paco most definitely was at that time.

When Paco moved to the premises he is now in, he sold El Pilón to a young Englishman named Christian, and his Spanish wife Mari-Lou. They are a really nice couple and have made a complete success there, by cooking more of an international cuisine, rather than trying to compete with Paco's typical Spanish menu.

The Spanish seem to have a tendency for opening museums, celebrating various foods and drinks, and Competa is no exception to this. I have the feeling that local government grants could play a big incentive in this.

If you walk down the slope from El Pilón, and turn right towards the communal swimming pool, you will find El Museo del Vino, (The Museum of Wine). This is a very nice, and very interesting bar, which also sells tapas and raciones (larger tapas). But, because of its status as a museum, it also sells different types of local produce and handicrafts, as well as the local wine. It does have a restaurant attached, where you can also dine on proper meals if you wish

There is also a Museo del Jamón (Museum of Ham) in the village, although I have never been in there, so cannot tell you anything about it. Towards the lower part of the village however, there was nearly a Museo del Aceite (Museum of the Olive). I say nearly, because this was once, an enormous old building, which used to be an olive mill, complete with much of the original equipment, including the huge grinding stones, the rush mats, and lots of lovely old wooden beams. I heard, at the time, that it was possibly for sale, and so I arranged to go and look at it, along with a very good Spanish friend. Our idea was to turn it into a small hotel and restaurant, whilst keeping as much as possible, of the old building, its stone walls, wooden beams, and of course the olive mill equipment.

Our plan was to apply for a local government grant, to turn the whole place into a Museo del Aceite. But, I am sorry to say that our plans did not come to fruition, mainly for two reasons, firstly, the mill was owned by the village as a whole, as it had always been used as a communal olive mill, this meant that the local council, and mayor, would have to vote on this change of use, in our favour, which for some reason unbeknown to us, never came about. The building, as far as I know, is still there, still unused, and rapidly falling into disrepair. I did hear a rumour that someone else, with a little more political influence than us had other plans for it, but of course, rumours like this are rife, especially in little villages like Competa, who knows?

There is of course, one hotel already in Competa, which is the Hotel Balcón de Cómpeta. It is a nice, reasonably big hotel, with 26 double rooms and 8 bungalows. It has a fine restaurant, two swimming pools, one just for children, a function room and bar, and a lovely terrace with marvellous views right over the countryside. The hotel is run by José López Franquelo, who was born in Competa, and David Avenell, an Englishman from Oxford, who now lives in Competa.

I first met José López Franquelo, some years ago, before the hotel was built, when he used to own a little restaurant called Franquelo's, just off the main square, next to the church. It was a tiny place, with the majority of the seating, outside in a small alleyway, but Franquelo, as he is known, would always make you welcome, and more importantly, he knew how to make his customers feel special. He would tell you what specials he had that day, and if he thought you wasn't too sure, he would say, 'you tell me how you like it cooked, and we will do it, special for you', I have seen him fill many tables like this. He worked hard then, and as far as I know, he is still working hard. He deserves all the success he gets.

Lastly, my good friend Paco, all you have to do to find his place, is walk past the Hotel Balcón de Cómpeta, keep going up the hill and around the bend, and there it is on your right; Cortijo Paco. Paco designed the restaurant himself, and is rightly very proud of it. It is on two floors, with a marvellous open roof terrace at the top. The views from there are absolutely spectacular. You can see right down to the coast at Algarrobo. I love to sit up there at night and watch all the lights down on the coast, twinkling and sparkling like a diamante crocodile. I remember also sitting up there one night, when it was the night of the bonfires, just after the grape harvest, and watching all the little fires burning brightly in the blackness of the hills.

Paco is a self taught chef, and a most excellent one at that, his specialities are mostly game type dishes, but he also cooks a fine selection of fish and most other dishes. His own personal favourites are sweet things, deserts. I remember him joining my wife and I, at our table one night, and asking us to try a new dish he just created, it was Berenjenas con Miel (Aubergines with Honey). The aubergines are sliced thinly, a little thicker than potato crisps, and then deep-fried, and then the honey (a dark one), is poured over them. I am not a lover of very sweet things, but to watch Paco's face light up as he tucked into this dish, was like watching a little boy eating ice cream. A delight. Going to Competa? Then Paco's is a must!

Another must of course, is Canillas de Albaida, which is a small village just 4 kms away from Competa, where the nearby-protected area of the Acantilados de Maro Nature Reserve, is situated. This is surrounded by high mountains of which the Atalaya and Verde mountains dominate a landscape of pine and oak trees; the habitat of eagles, mountain goats and wild boars. In the river valleys, grapes, olives and tropical fruits are grown. The village itself doesn't have the vibrant life going on that Competa has, but it is well worth seeing for its magnificent maze of streets, twisting and winding at different levels. Calle Estación is the main thoroughfare, with numerous steep narrow alleys running off it on either side.

El Callejón de Araceli is one of those, which attracts most attention, as it is barely possible to squeeze through between the houses on either side. All the streets lead to the Plaza del Ayuntamiento e Iglesia, the traditional village square. From here it is possible to see the shrine to Santa Ana, which dates from the sixteenth century. Remains of the original stucco lie below the layers of whitewash. Legend says that under the shrine to Santa Ana, in the highest and oldest part of the village, there is a tunnel that nobody has ever found. This passage, according to tradition, leads to the riverbed and was used by the Moors to fetch water. Opposite the shrine is a flat area known as "El Allaná" where, at barely 20 metres in height, it is possible to see the outline of doors in the rock. Popular lore tells that these doors were once real and later blocked up. A winding track, Arabic in origin and made of stone, leads to the spot known as Las Cuestas. There is also a stone bridge spanning the Rivers Cájules and Turvilla.

The nature reserve is particularly nice for a picnic beside the river. There is a picnic area set out there, along with showers, which I believe local schools use. Frances and I took a picnic there one day, and settled down beside the river, not far from the shower cubicles. We had just laid everything out, and poured ourselves two cold glasses of wine, when we suddenly heard the sound of machinery starting up. I looked around to see clouds of white dust belching out of the shower cubicles, and heading our way. Of all the days we could have picked, we picked the day when the local council had decided to fumigate the showers! Needless to say, we quickly packed up our picnic, and headed as far away as possible.

As you head further up stream, it is as if you were a million miles from any other civilisation, in a complete, silent world of your own, the only sounds being those of overhead birds and the running waters of the river. We just went to make a new start on our picnic when we heard another noise, this time it was the clip clopping sound of a donkey's hooves on the rocks near the river. An ancient man came through the undergrowth towards us, leading his donkey by its reins. He looked about ninety years old, so dark that his skin was like burnt leather. He held out his hands towards us as he saw us, 'oh no', I thought, he looks mad, and I was sure that he was going to start begging from us. We immediately started to pack up our picnic things yet again, but by this time the man was with us. I looked up at him as his outstretched hands reached towards me. I was ready to push him away if need be, or at the very least, shout at him and tell him to go away, but then I saw what it was that he had in his hands, he had two handfuls of fresh walnuts, which he was offering to us. He gave us the walnuts with a big smile and went on his way, just a friendly gesture, which I am sorry to say, we seem to have lost the art of here in the UK.

Chapter 10

Here we are, back where we started, in Nerja once again. If you take a little piece of all the other towns and villages I have spoken about, you will probably find at least one piece from each of them somewhere in Nerja, but you will never find a piece of Nerja in any of them. This is not to say that any of those places that we have visited, are not beautiful places in their own right, because they all are. But Nerja, has something special all of its own, whilst remaining in essence, still a village, it has the feel about it, of a cosmopolitan city.

I have written much, about the Spanish culture and food, but whilst still retaining its earthy Spanish flavours, Nerja, has managed to integrate with the many different cultures of its visitors, settlers, and even its early invaders, from the Moors, to the British, the Germans and Scandinavians, and of course, the more recent Africans, Asians, and Chinese.

If you go to the weekly street market in Nerja, or indeed any of the other towns and villages I have mentioned, you will find many of the stalls now being run by Africans, selling not just African produce, which many of them do, from beautiful wooden carvings, to hand made jewellery and clothing, but also, goods that were previously only sold by local Spanish people, such as watches, clothing, and electrical goods.

And if you are looking for somewhere different for a meal out, just take a brief walk around the town. You will find everything from Thai, to Greek, Chinese, German, French, Italian, Mexican, English, Irish, and of course, Spanish. If you can't find what you are looking for in Nerja, then I can only assume that you must be from another planet.

Personally, I always try to avoid restaurants that advertise "International Cuisine". There is nothing wrong in this of course, especially if it is home cooked, and it can give you a much wider choice of menu. But my reason for thinking like this, is that some years ago, a business partner and myself, opened a wine bar and restaurant in North London, and to be perfectly honest, neither of us had a great deal of knowledge about how to run a place like that, and even worse, I just about knew how to cook a few dishes, but my partner, couldn't even boil an egg. So what did we do? We got in touch with a catering firm, who supplied us packs of frozen, ready made meals, which were labelled "International Cuisine", They wasn't bad, but they certainly wasn't first-class either, and most definitely not the sort of thing I would want to order in a restaurant today. I am not saying that every restaurant that advertises "International Cuisine" is serving up frozen meals, but it does make me pause for thought, every time I see those words.

Special meals for kids. How many times have we all seen this? And Nerja is no exception to this. I have seen many restaurants, especially the more touristy type, around the centre, which offer special meals for kids, or children's menu, and I am always amazed at how many people seem to fall for this. Or maybe they don't really fall for it at all, maybe it is just another way of mummy and daddy having the most expensive meal on the menu, whilst palming little Rupert and Jessica, off with a plate of animal shaped chips and baked beans, for about 3 Euros? Whatever the answer, I don't agree with it. You don't see Spanish families treating their children as if they are from another planet, they all sit down together and eat the same food together. I have seen little Spanish children, who look no older than three or four years old, happily tucking into a plate of deep fried baby calamari, complete with heads, eyes and tentacles. Can you imagine the average British child allowing such food to even touch their plate?

When my son was very young, I encouraged him to eat the same food that I ate. I never forced him to eat anything, but I used to offer him a piece of mine, and slowly but surely he came to try, and to like, almost all foods. He now does the same with his children, and do you know what my grandson's favourite food in Nerja, is at the moment? Clams in white wine, cream and garlic sauce, and he is nine years old.

But, of course, the choice is yours, if you want special meals for the kids, then you will find this in Nerja, but if you want them to eat good healthy food, and to grow up to appreciate it, then you will have no trouble finding this also in Nerja.

There are other things for kids to do in Nerja, besides eating of course. The main thing that nearly all kids love to do, is mess around in the sea, and on the beach, and Nerja has so many different beaches, along its shore, from small rocky secluded coves, to wide expanses of beach. I have already covered Burriana Beach, but at the western end of town, there is another wide and very popular beach, called Torrecilla. There are not so many restaurants and bars at Torrecilla Beach, but it is still an excellent beach, and the recipient of a blue flag, which is awarded to beaches for safety, cleanliness, and good bathing conditions. Both Torrecilla and Burriana, are very safe beaches for children, as they both slope gently into the sea, and the sand it quite fine on both of them. So much so, that you often see sand sculptures made up, especially on Torrecilla.

During the Spring, April or May, after most of the families and children have left the beach in the early evening, you often get surfers using Torrecilla Beach, as this particular stretch of beach seems to catch the wind more at that time of year. I have often stood on the terrace of my apartment, which overlooks this beach, and watched the surfers in the warm red glow of the Nerja sunset. Many of them are very good, and really worth a visit to this beach to watch.

As well as the beaches, and depending on one's age of course, there is also horse riding, which children as well as adults can do. This is available from several stables, mostly about fifteen minutes away, in the Frigiliana area. You can find phone numbers and details advertised in the local magazines and newspapers, which you can pick up, free of charge, in most estate agent's doorways.

There are also two very good aqua parks reasonably close by, which most children always seem to enjoy, the first being Aqua Velis, which is about 12 miles to the west of Nerja in Torre del Mar, and the other is Aqua Tropic, which is in Almuñecar, about 25 minutes to the east of Nerja.

One of the simplest and cheapest ways to keep young children amused, is to buy them a fishing net and a bucket, and let them do some fishing for the little fish and crabs, which you can find in the rocky coves between Nerja's main beaches. It is a joy to see their faces light up when they do manage to actually catch something. You do have to keep an eye on them though, and make sure that they wear something suitable on their feet, to protect them from the sharp rocks. For those a little older, these little coves can be excellent for snorkelling.

But what am I telling you things like this for? If you are old enough, and wise enough, to be able to read this, then you should also be wise enough to be able to look after your own children, without being told what to do. In my opinion, we have enough of this sort of thing already in the UK, with our nanny state telling us what we should and should not do all the time. In a recent heat wave here in the UK, they even told us, that if we wanted to keep cool, then we should avoid the sun, put our feet in cold water, and splash cold water on our faces. Isn't that just great advice? We would never have thought of such little gems of wisdom without loveable old nanny to guide us would we?

There are, in my opinion, two main reasons why so many people go to Spain for their holidays, the first is obviously the weather, and the second, is for the freedom it allows us. For two short weeks, the average holiday-maker can get away from all the petty bureaucracy and rules that we have to endure in our daily lives within the UK.

You can sit outside a restaurant or a bar for as long as you want, without being bothered by waiters, like you would be in the UK, asking if you are going to order anything else, otherwise they will have to bring you the bill, as other people are waiting for the table. And so many towns and cities in the UK won't even allow outside seating, let alone allow you sit and relax for as long as you want.

A few years ago, I used to be the proud owner of a classic 35 year old, Mercedes sports car, and spares for such cars are not very cheap, to say the least, but luckily for me, I had managed to find somewhere, not too far from London, where I lived, where a particular spare I needed, could be found, so I set out with my wife and finally found this charming little village where the spares shop was located. By the time we got there, we were both rather hungry, so we decided to have some lunch in the village pub, which advertised "Good Pub Grub". We looked at what was on offer on the large blackboard, where it was chalked up, and then went to the bar to order, only to be told by the barmaid, who seemed to delight in the fact that it was too late for food, as it was now ten minutes past two, and they stopped serving at two. She made sure that she had served our drinks up first, we wasn't too late for that! I then asked her if they had any sandwiches, but of course, I should have known better, 'no food after two' she snapped, 'not even a bag of crisps?' I asked. Oh yes, we could have them, she said, but then promptly found out that the only crisps they had were some ridiculous flavour, like "lamb with mint flavour". Needless to say, we told her to forget it, drank our drinks and left, not feeling at all happy.

Scenes like that just do not happen in Spain. If a restaurant or a bar is open, they will serve you with food or whatever you want. I have been in restaurants in Nerja when the staff have cleared up, and I was the last person in there, and suddenly a customer comes in and orders a meal. They do not complain, that is what they are there for, to serve you. And they do it with a smile.

As for driving, it is like driving in a different world, to what the average driver from the UK has to endure. Firstly, you can fill your car up with fuel for less than half of what you would pay in the UK, and this is not because the wages are so much less there than in the UK, it is because their taxes are so much lower. No country in Europe pays as much tax and VAT as we do in the UK. Having filled your car up with fuel, you drive out onto the main road, and I am talking about the main N340 coastal road, which runs all the way from Nerja to Velez Malaga in the west, to Almuñécarr in the east. The driving is just so relaxed, if someone toots their horn at you, it is to warn you of something, it is not used as an act of aggression, as it is in the UK.

So as you poodle along, taking in the beautiful scenery, you suddenly see a beach that looks inviting. What do you do? You just pull over, right onto the beach and get out, leaving your car where it is. No gaunt looking official in a peaked cap is going to stride up to you and start threatening you with fines so big, that they are sometimes greater than the value of your vehicle. I remember the first time that I actually did this, and I stood my ground for a few minutes, looking around me, waiting to see if someone was going to come darting out from behind a bush, and rush towards me, pen and pad poised, ready to strike. When I did spot a man a little way off, waving to me, I thought 'oh no, here we go again,' but then I realised that he was the owner of a nearby chiringuito, and all he was doing was welcoming me.

Not all parking is quite that easy, especially in the peak summer months in Nerja town itself, you sometimes have to drive around for a considerable time to find somewhere to park, but all street parking is free, as it should be. The only place where you have to pay, is the few street around Burriana Beach, where you pay under one Euro to park all day, or the town's car park, where the charge is much the same. The parking wardens here are also something of a welcome change, from the parking wardens we have come to accept in Britain. Firstly, they are not dressed like Nazi Storm troopers, as ours are, and they actually smile at you! When was the last time you ever saw a parking warden smile at you in the UK? The last time I remember this was when one issued me with a parking ticket, and it was more of an evil grin than a smile. But what I find really nice, is the fact that the parking wardens here, are all disabled people, and a large percentage of what they collect in parking fees, goes towards their wages. So if you can, please try to do as I do, and give them a little extra than the meagre few centimos that they ask for the day's parking. They are really worth it believe me, and they will keep a special eye out on your car for this.

Even the police act differently to how they do in the UK. They do not persecute motorists just for the sake of it. If someone is speeding, they will go after them and can fine them on the spot, but there are no speed cameras, sitting there at the side of almost every road, like tin money making machines, as there are in the UK. And police don't stop every motorist who might have had just one beer to cool themselves down, either, they pay much more attention to those motorists whom they suspect of driving under the influence of drugs, rather than the odd drink, something the police in the UK should consider more.

I was talking to one of the people I know, who lives up in the mountain village of Competa, and I asked him how he got on with the local police, especially as he lives out in the countryside, regularly drives into the village, and is not unknown to partake of a drink or two, upon his visits. He told me that although he never gets drunk, he would quite often be classed as over the limit, by UK standards. So, I asked him, had he ever been pulled up by the police then, on his way home at night, and what he told me, was the difference between the UK's petty bureaucratic laws, rules and regulations, and the way his local police-force handled it. The police had indeed pulled him over on several occasions, they made him get out of his car to see if he could walk a straight line, and talk without slurring, and then, when they were reasonably sure that he wasn't drunk and incapable of driving, they actually escorted him back to his house, with them driving in front of him, and him following them behind in his car. Now this is what I call common sense, and it also builds a good relationship between the local police and the community, which again, seems something the police in the UK are not capable of, or very interested in.

If you are asking yourself at this point, why I am going on about the UK so much, in a book that is supposed to be about Spain, and Nerja in particular, there is a simple reason, and that is because I am trying to point out the differences between the two cultures, and what makes so many Brits want to holiday, and indeed, live and settle in this area of Spain.

Years ago, we used to hear of the Spanish culture of "mañana" (tomorrow), which unfortunately, and wrongly, gave the Spanish bad publicity, insinuating that they were a lazy race, who put off doing almost everything, by saying they would do it mañana. This simply isn't true. I have dealt with many Spanish business people over the years, and I can personally vouch for their efficiency, and get up and go attitude to work in general.

Another misconception is the "Spanish Builder" and "Spanish Plumber" syndrome. I am just about fed up with hearing those phrases used in connection with bad work. Working, as I did, with estate agents in Nerja, I got to view a great deal of properties, and you can believe me when I tell you that the general standard of workmanship is nothing less than first class. I laid on the beach once, in La Heradura, and watched a gang of Spanish workmen, putting the finishing touches to some apartments across the road. The temperature was in the region of 35°C. This was mid afternoon, when the general misconception is, that all Spanish workmen are having their siesta. Well, these guys certainly wasn't, they were happily working away and making all the noise and shouting, that is generally associated with builders of any nationality. I had the chance some months later, to view these apartments, and they were absolutely first class in every way.

Earlier on, I touched on a recent heatwave that we had in the UK. Schools were being closed, railway lines buckling with the heat, tarmac melting on the roads, hosepipe bans, tube stations being closed, and the motorways coming to a standstill, with cars overheating and breaking down everywhere. Television and newspapers had articles about it every day, how people were struggling to keep cool, and what they were wearing, and eating, and drinking. If you were an alien from another planet who had just arrived here on earth, you could have been excused for thinking that this must have been the prelude to the end of the world. But it wasn't, of course, it was just Britain, "sweltering" and moaning as usual, as the temperature reached "a record breaking 31°C". This was mid July, what did we expect, 18°C? And, more importantly, can you imagine a bunch of British builders, working out in the full sunshine, in the same heat that it was that day there in La Heradura? Their union would no doubt tell them that they should down tools, and only work when a temperature of no more than 21°C was reached, and even then, only when and if, they were supplied with protective clothing and vats of factor 56 sun block cream

This, of course, is just another example of the difference between the Spanish and the British. While Spanish builders get on with it, we find that so many British builders find something to gripe about. We have all had them, when they come into your house to give you an estimate for a job, be it building or plumbing, or electrical work, they will nearly always use the term 'what cowboy did this lot then?' and, 'there's not a lot I can do with this apart from ripping it all out and starting again'. If so many British builders say these things all the time, then what does that say for British building in general? Not a lot does it! So next time you hear the phrase Spanish builders, being used in a derogatory way, don't just take it as a fact, look for yourself, and then stand up for their excellent workmanship.

Chapter 11

One thing we all love to do when it is hot, and that is have a drink, whether it is alcoholic, or fruit juice, or just plain water, we cannot survive without it. And Nerja has more than its fair share of watering holes, from traditional bars and restaurants, to pavement cafes, and even a couple of English and Irish, pubs. The one thing that you do not find there are people walking along the street drinking. You might see the occasional child with a soft drink, but I cannot remember ever seeing adults walking along, drinking from cans of beer, as we do in the UK.

Two or three years ago, there was one particular corner in Nerja, which I used to call, English Corner. It is in Avenida Castilla Perez, which is the street that leads directly down from the town centre to Torrecilla Beach. There was one particular English style pub there called The Acorn Inn, and adjacent to this, on the next corner in fact, was another, smaller English style pub. And if this wasn't enough, just around the corner, was yet another one. I do not know the names of the two smaller ones, but they all certainly attract the Brits, especially if there is football on the TV. The Acorn Inn, used to have paintings of British footballers on the wall outside, and I must admit that I couldn't ever go past there without laughing to myself at the awful picture of David Beckham, which looked like it had been painted by a 6-year-old child. It's no wonder they have been painted over now, although I do quite miss not seeing them. If you like British beer and watching football on the big screen, then these pubs are a must for you, although I do believe the Acorn Inn has recently changed its format somewhat.

Just around the corner from there, in Calle Malaga, another British style pub once stood. It was called The Speakeasy, and was run by a big guy named John, from East London. You couldn't miss this one, as if you walked past there in the morning when they were serving breakfast, you would see bottles of Daddy's Sauce and Heinz Tomato Ketchup, on every table outside. Not exactly enduring to Spanish culture is it? Thankfully, in my opinion, the Speakeasy is now closed (at the time of writing) and is up for sale.

In the centre of town are several Irish bars, such as Durty Nelly's and Irish Annie's, and The Irish Harp Bar, and I believe, a few more, but as I have never been in any of them, I cannot really tell you much about them, apart from the fact that they all sell Guinness. If you want to find them, just stop the first Irish person you see and ask them. If they don't know, then maybe you should ask one of the little people themselves?

So, having dealt, however briefly, with Guinness and Brown Ale, I once again return to the tipples I know best, which are, wines, spirits, and the somewhat lighter beers. But before I do, I must touch on probably one of the most well known, and best loved, Spanish drinks there is, which is Sangria. Women, especially seem to love this drink, probably because it is sweet, and most women seem to have a taste for sweeter things than men do. I must admit that I do not drink Sangria myself, as I do not like oranges, or many sweet things in general, but I love the look of it, served up in one of those big earthenware or glass jugs, with all the ice on top, it does look so refreshing on a hot day, but I think it can also be quite intoxicating as well, depending on the amounts of alcohol used. If you fancy making it yourself, here (following) is a recipe:

Classic Spanish Sangria

This is an authentic version of this very popular drink. You can add any fruit that you want, including tinned fruit, depending on your particular taste. This particular recipe is not diluted with lemonade or tonic water, but again, you can add them if you wish. Try to use a decent red wine, and either white rum, or dark, depending again on your taste.
Serves 6 people.

INGREDIENTS:
1 lemon
1 lime
1 orange
1 cup of rum
1/2 cup white sugar
1 (750 millilitre) bottle dry red wine
1 cup orange juice
DIRECTIONS:

Chill the fruit, rum, wine, and orange juice well. Slice the lemon, lime and orange into thin rounds and place in a large earthenware, or glass jug. Pour in the rum and sugar and stir well. Chill in refrigerator for 2 hours to fully develop the flavours. When ready to serve, crush the fruit lightly with a wooden spoon and stir in the wine and orange juice. Adjust sweetness to taste, and add some ice. Perfect for a warm afternoon by the pool!

Another drink, which is similar to Sangria, but not as sweet, is Tinto Verano (Red Summer) which is red wine with either lemonade or soda water. Many bars now do this drink in drought form, direct from the tap.

It is pronounced "Tinto Berr-arno". The letter "V" is always pronounced like a "B" in Spanish, such as Vaso (glass) is pronounced Baso. Un Vaso (a glass) is what we would call a tumbler type glass, if you want a glass of wine, this would be un copa de vino, pronounced "un copa de bino".

Another fallacy, which I am pleased to say, is at long last disappearing, is the fallacy of the so-called "Spanish Plonk". When it comes to wine, Spain produces some of the finest in the world. Years ago, French, seemed to be the only quality wine available, and the so called wine experts would look down their noses at the Spanish wines, labelling them as cheap Spanish plonk.

All wines are labelled according to the regions from where they are produced. There are so many types and tastes available in Spain, that it would be impossible to list them all here in just a small space, but here are a few of the main names.

Red Wine Regions: Rioja, Valdepeñas, La Mancha, Ribera del Duero, Toro, Priorat, Navarra, Cariñena, Jumilla, Bierzo, Almansa, Montsant, Campo de Borja, Castilla, Manchuela.

White Wine Regions: Penedès, Ribeiro Valdeorras, Rías Baixas, Rueda, Txacolí regions (Basque Country), Alella, Lanzarote.

Rosés: Navarra, Cigales, Utiel-Requena

Fortified Wines: Jerez (sherry), Montilla-Moriles, Malaga

Sparkling Wine: Cava

Sweet Wines: Montilla-Moriles (Pedro Ximenez), Valencia (Muscatel), Malaga (Pedro Ximenez.

Probably the most famous Spanish wine is Rioja which was the first Spanish wine region to obtain DO status in 1925. In 1991, it was promoted to DOCa (Qualified Designation of Origin), a higher category reserved for wines maintaining a proven consistency and quality over a long period of time.

Rioja DOCa is known primarily for its reds, although it also makes some excellent white wines, and rosés. Most bodegas still use their own formulas for blending red wines with at least three other types of grapes, the most important of which is Tempranillo, the noblest of the native Spanish vines. This grape gives the wines their elegance, concentration of aromas and complexity of flavours. It is this, as well as ageing in American oak barrels, which gives the wines such personality and individuality.

No one can tell you which wine you should drink, with what particular food; it is all down to personal taste. Although, reds are always associated with meat dishes, just as whites are with fish, but, I know many people, including myself, who always drink red wine with a seafood paella. It is also quite common in Spain, for certain red wines to be served chilled, and not at room temperature, as we tend to do in the UK, but I must say that this is usually associated with the very young red wines, which need to be drunk within a year of being produced, and not for aged Riojas.

When I was a young boy, and Christmas time came around, we often had family get togethers, where I would meet aunts and uncles, who I would never see again until the following Christmas. I always remember one aunt in particular, because she drank tiny glasses of a very dark drink called Sherry. I once tried a sip when no one was looking, and thought how disgusting it was. But, I thought, this was obviously what very old English ladies drank (my aunt was probably about 35 at the time). From that time, until quite recently, it seemed to disappear in prominence from the British drinking scene, becoming just a distant memory of days gone by.

Now, of course, Sherry is slowly but surely, making a comeback. Not so much the dark sweet Sherry that my aunt drank, but the pale, dry type, known as Fino. It is even considered quite cool, to have a glass of chilled Fino Sherry, which is also, a perfect accompaniment to tapas, especially shellfish.

Jerez, the area where Sherry is made, also makes Brandy, which I personally consider to be the best in the world. Brandy de Jerez is made by the Sherry houses centred around the city of Jerez de la Frontera in the southwest corner of Spain. Virtually all Brandy de Jerez, however, is made from wines produced elsewhere in Spain, primarily from the Airen grape in La Mancha and Extremadura, as the local Sherry grapes are too valuable to divert into Brandy production. Nowadays most of the distilling is likewise done elsewhere in Spain using column stills. It is then shipped to Jerez for ageing in used Sherry casks in a solera system similar to that used for Sherry wine. A solera is a series of large casks, called butts, each holding a slightly older spirit than the previous one. When brandy is drawn off (racked) from the last butt (no more than a third of the volume is removed) it is replenished with brandy drawn from the next butt in line all the way down the solera line to the first butt, where newly distilled brandy is added. This system of racking the brandy through a series of casks blends together a variety of vintages (some soleras have over 30 stages) and results in a speeding up of the maturing process.

Basic Brandy de Jerez Solera must age for a minimum of six months, Reserva for one year and Gran Reserva for a minimum of three years. In practice, the best Reservas and Gran Reservas are frequently aged for 12 to 15 years. The lush, slightly sweet and fruity notes to be found in Brandy de Jerez come not only from ageing in Sherry casks, but also from the judicious use of fruit-based flavour concentrates and oak essence (boise).

Another drink that has risen in prominence in Spain, over the last few years, is beer, even surprisingly, amongst women, and older people, whom we normally associate with drinking wine.

I am sure that most of you know the Spanish word for beer, but for those who don't, it is Cerveza, which should be pronounced "Serv-etha". So if you want a glass of beer, it would be Un Vaso de Cerveza, a bottle of beer is un botella de Cerveza, pronounced un "bot-eaya" de Cerveza. And if you want a drought beer, you ask for Una Cana, pronounced "Oona Can-ya".

Having armed yourself with a little knowledge of what drinks are available, and how to pronounce and order them, all you have to do next, is find your perfect place for drinking them.

When in Nerja, I usually like to start the evening off in a nice, light atmosphere, and Marisqueria La Marina is exactly that. It is situated on the west side of town, in Avenida Castilla Perez, and is a seafood tapas bar and restaurant, with tables inside and more outside by a small square, where there is waiter service. I like to start off with usually, a couple of finos or beers, each accompanied of course, by free tapas, such as a seafood salad or a plate of gambas (prawns). The drinks here are very cheap, as too is the price of the main meals, should you be tempted. I usually am, and normally end up ordering one or two pinchos de jibia (skewers of baby cuttlefish), which have been cooked on the barbecue grill, with a little garlic. They are delicious!

If you go early evening, at about 7.30pm, it is still not too crowded, and you can usually manage to grab a stool at the bar. There is one problem with Marisqueria La Marina, and that is that they do not have enough stools to go all the way around the huge horseshoe shaped bar. They have about a dozen, when they should have 40 at the least, but with the amazing quality of the food, and unbelievable prices, I'm not complaining.

Just around the corner from Marisqueria La Marina, is a lovely little bar - restaurant, called La Tahona (the bakery), which is in Plaza Garcia Caparros. It is quite difficult to find, as it is located in ground floor premises of an apartment block, but once you do manage to find it, it is well worth the effort. It is run by two young brothers, Alejandro and Fernando. There are tables in the plaza outside, plus a dining room at the back of the bar, which is imaginatively painted to resemble an outside courtyard. The food here is very good, and reasonably priced, and the free tapas, are as you would expect, first class, with something different being on offer every night. If you are a meat lover, then this is just the place to start your evening off.

Since I started this book, and decided to re-write it, one of the main things to have happened in Spain, is as I have previously mentioned, the smoking-ban has come into place there. Many people have been put off going to Spain again because of this, but as a smoker myself, I can honestly say that the ban has not affected the average smoker's lifestyle to a great degree. As we all know, the temperatures in Spain are very pleasant for almost all the year, which means that sitting outside to have a smoke doesn't affect one like it does in the cold and damp UK.

Over the last few years, tapas bars seem to have taken over from restaurants, as the main choice for an evening out, especially it would seem, in Nerja. With more and more tapas bars springing up and competing for business, the tapas have grown exceedingly better, and with the outcome of the smoking-ban, an outdoor area is a must, so in one way, the ban has helped the smoker, especially in Nerja.

Whereas most of the old restaurants and bars are still centred around the centre of town, the new tapas bars seem to be springing up on the western side of town, in the area behind Plaza Tuti Fruti. They are relatively easy to find, all you need to do is find this area and listen to the ever increasing sounds of the locals chatting; the louder is gets, the closer you are! There is one bar there called Sevilianos 2, which is in Calle Chaparil; its sister bar Sevilanos 1 is in the centre of town. This bar has been here for a couple of years maybe, and is a very friendly place, serving excellent food and drink. Almost next door to Sevilanos 1 is one of the newer bars, called Candela. This only thing I do not like about Candela is their tables, which are very tall and set on central metal bases, and quite easily tipped over, which a young boy did when I was last there, narrowly missing me with all the drinks as they shattered on the floor next to me. Just across the street from Candela, are two more relatively new bars. One I have yet to go into, but the other one is called Taller de tapa, and has a large outside area and again, excellent tapas. One of my favourite tapas here is a mixture of fried fish, served in a paper cone, which almost reminds me of fish and chips wrapped in paper, like we buy it in the UK.

The village atmosphere of Nerja, means that it is almost impossible to take a short stroll around the town without bumping into someone you know. So many holiday makers, and ex-pats, insist on having televisions, so that they will not have to miss their favourite TV shows and soaps, but believe me, the gossip that you pick up from all the different people you bump into on your travels around the town, can quite often put Coronation Street and Eastenders, into the shade. A bar or a shop is closed, and the first thing you hear is that the owner went bust and did a runner, owing everyone huge amounts of money. The next person you bump into tells you that is completely untrue, the owner in fact suddenly dropped down dead, while the next person tells you that he sold out, and new people are taking over from next week. All quite harmless in its way I suppose, unless of course the poor guy happened to owe you money, then I suppose this sort of gossip could cause trouble.

Something like this happened to me about a year or so ago. I hadn't been to Nerja for some months, and so I made my way along Calle Carabeo, to pay one of my usual nocturnal visits to a bar there, called Sharp's Piano Bar, which was run by a good friend of mine named Tony Sharp, who played marvellous jazz on his beautiful Steinway grand piano.

It was about 11pm, a time when Tony's bar would normally be quite buzzing with customers. But as I approached the bar, I noticed that his usual neon sign above the door was not switched on, and neither were the wrought iron gates open. This was a Saturday night, so I knew it wasn't Tony's closing night, and then I noticed the white paper sign, stuck in the small window beside the door. It was a hand written letter, signed by Tony, which said *"I am closing this bar on 4th July* (I am not sure of the exact date) *and will never open it again. I would like to thank all my customers and friends for their support and friendship over the years, and I look forward to seeing you all again in the next life"*.

What on earth did he mean by that? I thought. I knew that he had been having a lot of problems with a neighbour, who didn't appreciate his piano playing, even though he was already there playing, long before she had moved in. And because of this neighbour, the local police had stopped him from playing any more. This of course meant that his takings in the bar, dropped considerably, after all, how many people want to go to a piano bar where the piano cannot be played?

So Tony told me that he now wanted to sell the bar, and I agreed to advertise it for him on my website, which I did. But, after almost a year without receiving any interest in it all, Tony started to look a little more worried each time I saw him. He had by then taken up writing, and said that he wanted to get out of the bar business altogether, buy a little house somewhere and concentrate on writing novels.

Quite a few of the people I knew in Tony's had expressed their concern about him in the past few months, saying how he had lost interest in the place etc. So, you can imagine what I thought, when I saw that hand written note in Tony's window.

At the far end of his bar, was a beautiful little terrace that looked down, over the jagged rocks to the sea below. Tony loved a drink, and he had gone there, to his little terrace one night, and sat there alone with his thoughts, nursing a bottle of his best whiskey. After an hour or two of deep contemplation, he wrote the note and stuck it into his window. He then returned to the terrace, and squeezed the last remaining dregs from the whiskey bottle, took one final look round his once beloved bar, and then threw himself over the balcony, onto the rocks below, killing himself instantly.

None of this was true of course, it was thankfully, just a figment of my overworked imagination, but I did think at the time, that maybe, just maybe, it could possibly be true. After all, why should he mention seeing everyone in the next life? I must admit, that both my wife and I were almost in tears. Poor Tony, we thought, poor, poor, Tony. But I, being a bit more resolute than my wife, and still at that time, thinking that he had jumped, quickly pulled myself together. 'Look' I said, 'moping around like this is not going to help anyone, the last thing he would have wanted, is to see us like this, so I suggest that we go somewhere else, and have a drink, and dedicate it to Tony.'

But where? I was so used to going to Tony's for a late drink, all the other bars I used were for earlier drinking hours (at this particular time). My wife and I started to walk back in the direction of our apartment, deciding that we would have a drink at the first bar we came to that was open. It was then that I suddenly remembered a little bar in a narrow back street, that we had been to just once, a couple of years before.

Maybe we might bump into someone we knew from Tony's, who could tell us exactly what had happened? We were not far from it, so we made a little detour towards the end of Calle Pintada, and sure enough there it was, in Calle Nueva, the bar, just as I remembered it, called La Posada Iberica, which is just about as genuine Spanish as you can get. Small, with wood panelling and wrought iron grills on the windows, a few stools at the bar, and more around large wooden barrels that are scattered around the room. The place is mostly for drinking and the free tapas, but there is a small dining room in the back section, where I am told, they serve very good food.

There are different types of jamons (hams) hanging from the wooden beams, which they specialise in, hence the name, which denotes a type of jamon from that area. But there wasn't any of the old crowd from Tony's, in fact almost everyone that goes in this particular bar is Spanish, not that that should be such a surprise, after all, Nerja is in Spain. The reason I say this, is because nearly everyone that went in Tony's was British.

We had a drink and like we said, dedicated it to Tony, wherever he was. A couple of drinks later, and we had a real treat coming our way, for the owner suddenly took down a guitar from off a shelf and started to play and sing Flamenco, and he was surprisingly good. He ended with a Flamenco version of John Lennon's, Imagine, which is a particular favourite of mine, and I always think to be, a very sad song, especially on that night, with the thoughts of Tony still very strong in our minds.

What was really strange, was that for the next couple of weeks, I looked for anyone I knew that used to go into Tony's bar, in the hope that I could find out the truth once and for all, but neither my wife nor I saw a single person whom we used to see in there, and yet, as I said earlier, whenever anything happens in Nerja normally, the whole town seems to know about it, and is talking about it. The mystery did eventually unfold, which I will tell you about later.

La Posada Iberica is now one of my favourite bars in Nerja, unfortunately, the owner who played the guitar and sang that night, no longer runs it. Apparently, his wife become very ill, which made it very difficult for him to work in the bar and also take care of his wife, so he rented it to a girl named Silvia, who worked for him, and is from Argentina. Silvia now runs it, along with her husband, Paco, who works as a car mechanic during the day, even though he is often working in the bar until the early hours of the morning. I have never seen two people constantly smile as much as Silvia and Paco, a really lovely couple, whom, I am pleased to say, run La Posada Iberica along exactly the same lines as the previous owner, and now occasionally employ Paco Gumersindo, who is singer and guitarist whom I have already spoken about, to play and sing there on Saturday nights.

Speaking of genuine and old-fashioned bars in Nerja, there is one which is very close to the church in Plaza cavana, is a small bar, bearing the name "Cavana". This is another true Spanish bar, with authentic atmosphere, a very dark interior, and reasonably good tapas, but not free I am afraid, but you do get occasional music in there, which is free, and it also stays open quite late.

As so many new bars are now springing up, as previously mentioned, are mostly very good, there are also some that call themselves tapas bars, and offer dishes that are about as close to real tapas, as meat pie and two veg.

One such place is a very large, new building, which is also very close to the church. I won't bother to name it, as I wouldn't want anyone going there on my recommendation. I decided to try it out, a few months after it first opened. It is waiter service, and the waiters expect you to order all the dishes you might want, in one foul swoop. Who on earth knows how many drinks you might be having or how long you might be staying until you have actually tried the first dish? I certainly wish I had, for the first dish I was served up with, was supposed to be Albondigas (meatballs) in a rich tomato sauce. I ended up with four brown bullets with something, which tasted and looked like a poor imitation of tomato ketchup, squeezed all over them. I honestly cannot remember what other dishes I had in there, but I do remember the bill, when the surly waiter finally agreed to bring it to my table. It was enough to pay for a good meal in a decent restaurant, so be warned, try to order as little as possible, if you do ever have the misfortune to try out somewhere like this. You can always order more if it is good enough.

One good thing that did come out of going to that particular "tapas bar", was the fact that I met an old friend there, named Pieter, a Dutchman, who used to frequent Tony's. This guy is a real character, he looks about 50, but in reality, he is closer to 70. He is something of a hippy in his looks, with longish hair and a sometimes beard. He apparently used to have a big business in Holland, but then sold up one day and emigrated to Nerja, where he has been ever since.

Pieter has two main loves, the first being drink, and the second, women! He would often turn up at Tony's, looking already the worse for wear, and he would just not leave the women alone. There was no real harm in him, he would stand next to any woman he could get near, no matter if they were with their husbands or not, and he would start telling them what beautiful eyes they had, and how lovely they were. I have seen Tony get angry with him on several occasions, and ask him to leave, and he did without any arguments, he just smiled, waved at everyone, and left, only to return about half an hour later, having completely forgotten that he had just been thrown out.

One evening, Pieter showed up in Tony's with a pretty girl, probably about half his age, 'look everyone' he declared, 'this is Arkie, she is my girlfriend, isn't she beautiful? And I love her so much.' Tony remarked something like 'Good God, where did he get this one from? I hope her husband is not going to come charging in looking for her, and start a fight.'

But Arkie wasn't married, not that we know of anyway, and she stayed with Pieter for quite a time, about a couple of years I believe. They rented a house together in Carabeo, almost opposite Tony's bar, which was handy for them, as she seemed to like a drink almost as much as Pieter did. Arkie was Moroccan, quite slim and good looking, but I think she was something of a handful, so to speak, as she always seemed to be having arguments with Pieter. He didn't have arguments with her, he just looked at her and smiled all the time, and was always singing her praises, and telling everyone that he was going to marry her.

One night Arkie came into Tony's on her own; she had one drink and then left, saying that she was going to look for Pieter. She returned five minutes later, and said that her purse had been stolen or lost, with something like 25,000 Pesetas in it. Tony told her to go to the police and report it, but she wouldn't. She said she would find Pieter instead, he would know what to do. And of course, when she did eventually find Pieter and brought him back into Tony's, he did indeed know exactly what to do, he gave Arkie 25.000 Pesetas from his wallet. This caused quite a few raised eyebrows among Tony's clientele, as when Pieter did anything, he didn't care who saw or overheard, and he made quite a public display of counting the money out on Tony's bar, and handing it to his loved one. The impression I got, was that the majority of the people in Tony's that night, who had seen Arkie when she first came in, did not seem to recall seeing her with her purse in the first place. Tony was absolutely sure that if she had indeed had any money to start with, that it was almost a certainty that she had spent it on drugs. Who knows? I certainly don't.

I couldn't stop laughing another time, when Pieter came into Tony's looking very sad, and said that Arkie had left him. It wasn't this part of his story that made me laugh, it was when he told everyone in the bar that she had gone to live with another man, and worse still, that he knew the man. I tried to make him feel better, by telling him that maybe she wasn't with this man at all, that maybe she had just gone away for a few days to try to make him feel sorry for her. But Pieter insisted that Arkie was with this other man, 'he only lives around the corner', he said, 'and I can see Arkie's underwear hanging on his washing line, I should know, because I bought it for her'. What was so funny about this was the way in which Pieter told it and accepted it, as always with his usual smile on his face.

So when I saw Pieter that night in the so called tapas bar near the church, I was pleased to see him, and I wanted to know what he knew about the demise of Tony Sharp. But as usual, Pieter was a little bit slurry with his speech, and all he could manage to tell me was 'Oh yesh, Tony'sh ish clooshed now'. I knew the bloody place was closed, I wanted to know what had happened to Tony, but try as I might, I couldn't get anything more out of Pieter that night.

What I find really strange is that you can go somewhere, week in and week out, and think nothing more about it. In fact, sometimes you might even think to yourself, that it is only that same old place once again, but, when that place closes, you suddenly find that you really miss it, exactly as I did when I found Tony's closed. But worse still, I now found myself on a mission, to find out what happened to him. I just couldn't understand the fact that of all the people I used to know in there, I now wasn't seeing any of them, apart from Pieter of course. Where could they all have gone, they couldn't have all jumped over the balcony alongside Tony surely? Or could it be one of those strange alien abduction stories that we occasionally read about in the newspapers, where people are beamed up by a strange beam of light, into the mother ship? And this could be the reason of course, why they hadn't abducted Pieter along with all the others, the aliens would need people they could learn things from, and that would definitely rule Pieter out.

Hold on a minute I thought, how many drinks did I have in that last place? I was starting to let my imagination run away with me here. Then suddenly it hit me, what about Sinatra's Bar, that was a distinct possibility, and it is only five minutes walk away from Tony's, so off I went to Sinatra's, which is in Calle Los Huertos. I hadn't been to Sinatra's Bar for some years. I remember going in there with my wife a few years ago, and they were playing Elvis Presley on their music system. After listening to Elvis for about half an hour, my wife asked if they were going to play any Sinatra, to which the girl behind the bar said, 'no we're not, it's all right for you, but we have to listen to him all day'. So why didn't they rename the place then, and call it Presley's Bar? I don't see much point of having bar called Sinatra's, if they don't like playing his music in there.

Now, however, I think the place has changed ownership, for as I walked in that night, sure enough old Blue Eyes was singing his heart out, "The Summer Winds", I believe. There were only a few people at the bar; the majority were sitting at the tables, so I could see immediately that once again, there wasn't anyone I knew there. The new owners seemed to have made a vast improvement to the general atmosphere there; much more friendly and easy going, like a good bar should be, and the drinks were reasonably priced. So if you are looking for a bit of laid-back Sinatra, then this is the place for you.

As much as I like old Blue Eyes, it wasn't him that I was looking for that night, so I finished my drink and carried on with my quest, but I am afraid to say that I drew yet more blanks.

This was becoming like an obsession with me, I even dreamed about Tony's bar that night. In fact it was his cat, Tabsy that I dreamt about. Tony loved that cat; he even used to feed it with giant gambas (prawns), which even in Spain can be quite expensive, especially for a cat. If you went into the bar early evening, before the punters started arriving, you would often see Tony feeding Tabsy, and stroking and talking to it, like it was his long lost child. So you can imagine how he must have felt when one day, poor old Tabsy died. He had found Tabsy dead one morning, and was sure within his mind, that the cat had been poisoned, possibly by someone living very close to his bar, who didn't like music, and had a personal grudge against him. Tony was absolutely devastated, and still continued to talk about his darling Tabsy, whenever he got the chance.

One night, just before closing, the subject of Tabsy arose once again, and Tony told my wife and I, in all sincerity, that he had seen Tabsy's ghost, and if that wasn't enough, he had actually seen Tabsy playing his grand piano, well not actually playing it, but sort of walking across the keys, as if he were playing it. In my dream, Tabsy was actually sitting down and playing properly, in fact he was playing "Tenderly", which is an Oscar Peterson number, which Tony often used to play. My wife couldn't stop laughing the next morning when I told her about my dream, 'did the cat have dark glasses on and a cigarette dangling from his lips as well?' She laughingly asked.

She may well have laughed, but when I think of some of the characters I have met in Tony's, it is not totally inconceivable that maybe Tabsy might have worn dark glasses or smoked the occasional cigarette. It was like a magnet in there, for some of the weirdest characters you could hope to meet in Nerja. This is not to say that everyone who went in Tony's was weird, or even "characters" so to speak, many were just ordinary people who enjoyed listening to Tony playing the piano, and meeting other like minded people. But I must admit, I was fascinated by the characters, such as Pieter and Arkie, whom I have already spoken about.

I remember going in there one night, and seeing that there was a young Spanish guy, Raúl, working behind the bar. He would serve drinks while Tony was playing the piano. He spoke reasonably good English, and was very good at his job, but when Tony stopped playing and returned to the bar, Raúl suddenly burst into song, which was a little unsettling, as we hadn't been warned, and to have this guy, just inches from your face, suddenly burst into a bout of Flamenco singing without any accompaniment, did seem a little strange. When he finished, Tony encouraged everyone into a round of applause, and then told us that this was Raúl, and he came from a very poor family and was going into the army soon, so any little tips we could offer, would undoubtedly help him. While I didn't doubt Tony one bit about what he said, I have never liked the idea of being coerced into giving tips to anyone. I do not like it in restaurants, when they add a service charge to your bill, and then tell you that it is optional. We all know it is optional anyway, so why try to force us into paying it, by trying to make us feel mean if we don't? I think I gave Raúl some loose change anyway, as he was a good singer, but I didn't feel that I needed to be told this.

The best singer I have ever heard in Tony's was Michael Browne, a very good friend of mine, whom Tony accompanied on the piano, in a marvellous rendition of All My Tomorrows. This is such a lovely song, which Frank Sinatra used to sing, and Michael sang it so beautifully, that I saw people with tears in their eyes as they watched him perform it.

Another Michael, not to be confused with the singer, Michael Browne, was Tall Michael, as we called him. He was nearly seven feet tall, and came from Senegal. He sold watches and African statues and wonderful ebony carvings. Working outdoors most of the time made Michael even darker than he was normally, and in the dim light of Tony's, he often resembled one of his own ebony statues. My wife bought the occasional watch from him, more out of friendship than anything else, as you could often buy them from a market stall, cheaper than Michael was selling them in Tony's, but, as nice as he was, he was another one like Pieter, who was woman mad. He would sit himself down next to any woman who happened to be there, and just stare at them, as if he was madly in love with them. This did become a bit of a pain, when he tried it on with my wife, and we found that the only way out of this, without actually arguing with him, was to leave and go somewhere else.

One night however, he came in with a rather large English lady on his arm, which I was relieved at, as it meant that he wouldn't be bothering Frances that night then. They had several drinks together, and then he said something to the woman, and he left. When the woman ordered another drink, Tony asked her who was going to pay for the drinks that they had already had during the course of the evening, to which she replied that it was all right, as "The Chief" had just gone home to get some more money, and would be returning shortly. Tony didn't suffer fools gladly, and he told the woman in no uncertain terms, that he didn't know any "Chief" and if Michael didn't return, that she would be liable for paying for the drinks. She was obviously very embarrassed, and looked round for someone else to talk to, which just happened to be my wife and myself. 'Have you met the chief?' she asked, 'I'll introduce you to him when he returns if you like?'. I did feel sorry for her, and didn't have the heart to tell her that Michael wasn't a chief, and that he had a stall down the market selling watches. The poor woman eventually paid both her and Michael's bar bill and left Tony's as quietly as possible.

When Tony was finally stopped by the local police, from playing his piano, he found that he could still attract his old regulars, by engaging them in conversation and witty stories, and as an ex Oxford educated man himself, with a vast knowledge of most things, including politics, religion, history, and of course, music. It could sometimes be a pleasure to listen to him, I say sometimes, because I remember once, when he called out for everyone to be quiet and listen to this cassette tape that he was about to play. I couldn't believe it when I heard "The day war broke out" by Rob Wilton. Now this might have been funny in 1940, or whenever it was made, but it certainly didn't make me laugh, or anyone else that I could see, in Tony's bar in modern day Nerja. But this was unusual, normally Tony brought everyone together, and got them talking about issues that were sometimes funny, sometimes important, but nearly always, very entertaining.

I happened to tell Tony a story about myself one night; it was about the time that I used to own a wine bar-restaurant in North London. A fight had broken out in there one night, between two really heavy looking factions, involving something like a dozen or more very large men. Needless to say, I just couldn't stand by and see my place getting smashed to pieces, so I had to wade in and do my best to stop it before the whole place got wrecked, and I lost all my customers. God knows how I did it, but after a while I did manage to break it up, and get them to leave.

About half an hour later, a couple of really heavy looking guys came back into my bar, and said that the person who had been the main instigator of this fight, was now outside, and wanted to see me. Now I happened to know that these people, were well known members of a particular crime family, and the last thing I wanted to do, was to go outside, alone, and face this particular guy, who was, apparently, the leader of this family. But, it seemed that I didn't have a lot of choice in the matter, as I was "gently" guided out of my bar and into the street, where this guy sat in his car waiting for me.

He got out of the car as we approached him, and I honestly thought that he was either going to shoot me or stab me, but instead of anything like that, he grabbed my hand and started shaking it, and apologising to me at the same time. He said that he would pay for all the damage that they had caused, so that they could come in again without any hard feelings. All I really wanted to do was get out of this guy's clutches, and get back into the safety of my bar, so I told him not to worry about it. With that he gave me a big hug, and kissed me on both cheeks. As he did this however, a car drove past with a group of young guys in it, and one of them leaned out of his window and shouted out at us 'Bloody poufters.' With that, Mr Big and his boys quickly left me, got back into their car and sped away. I don't know if they did it out of embarrassment or whether they went after the other car. I didn't care really, as long as I was safe once again.

Tony thought this story was marvellous, and he got me to repeat it time after time to various people in the bar, with me embellishing on the actions and the sizes of the people involved, each time that I told it. I suppose it was a good story, in retrospect, but not one that I would fancy living through again.

Everyone knows that the Irish are particularly good story-tellers, and Tony's had its fair share of the Irish, including Big Patsy, who was marvellous at telling jokes. I called him Patsy Cotobro, as he would often tell me about a restaurant that he, his wife, and a number of other people, including Tony, often went to on a Sunday. The restaurant was in Cotobro, which is next to La Heradura. 'World class, world class', Patsy would say, 'ten courses, and you can't fault it'. Ten courses for a Sunday lunch? I couldn't believe it, no wonder Patsy was a big man! He would tell a story that would carry on for twenty minutes or more, making everyone believe that it was a true story he was telling, and then he would suddenly come to the punch line, and along with almost everyone else, fall about laughing, his big red face getting redder by the minute. Every Monday, which was Tony's day for closing, he, and several others would meet up and walk to Maro, which is quite an accomplishment, especially for people of their age, and who liked a drink as much as they did.

But, two Irish people in particular, stand out in my mind, and they were Berna and her husband Michael (yes another Michael). They were lovely people, always happy, and she knew everything that was going on in Nerja. They didn't live there full time, but they used to stay, and I think they still do, for about 4 or 5 months every year. Berna, is one of those people who has a regal air about her, she holds court in a room, drifting from one set of people to the next, always smiling, always with a glass in her hand, but never, ever, drunk, like someone from a different age, a more gentler time than that which we are now forced to live in.

And so, when my wife and I, at last bumped into Berna and Michael late one night in Nerja, we were delighted to see them, and knew that at long last, the mystery of Tony's disappearance would be drawing to a close. They couldn't stop laughing when we told them what I had suspected, about Tony throwing himself off the balcony, and about his suicide note. 'He's alive and well,' said Berna, 'and living up in Frigiliana.' She didn't have his phone number with her, but told me to give her a ring the next day, when she would be able to give it to us, 'he'll be pleased to hear from you' she said, as she guided us into Sinatra's Bar and sat us down, 'now what will you be having?' Asked Michael.

Needless to say, I did have something of a hangover when I awoke the following morning, but after a long relaxed breakfast on our terrace overlooking Torrecilla Beach, and taking in the beautiful fresh ozone smells of the sea, I soon started to recover. By midday, Frances had already got Tony's phone number from Berna, and was busy phoning him as I was showering, 'he wants us to go to see him at his house in Frigiliana' she shouted to me. That would be nice, I thought, 'when?' 'Now' she replied, 'he said we could go for a meal to a little place close to his house.'

Oh God, I thought, as much as I was looking forward to seeing Tony again, I was not exactly in the mood at this point, to start drinking yet again. My wife always has the perfect answer for problems like this, 'well it's simple isn't it', she said, 'all you have to do is regulate yourself, have one glass of wine and then say no to any more'. With expert advice like that to bandy about, she should be running Alcoholics Anonymous; she'd soon cure them all!

An hour later, I was driving out of Nerja, in the direction of Malaga, with the village of Frigiliana signposted just slightly off to our right. It is a nice drive up to the village, not too mountainous, and with lovely views all the way. It only takes ten to fifteen minutes to get there, but it can take as long again to find somewhere to park. My advice is to park at the bottom of the village, where there are several roads laid out as car parking areas. If you drive up into the village itself, the roads do get very narrow and almost impossible to park in, and can be very confusing if you are not familiar with the layout of the village.

This particular day was, as usual, very hot, and walking from that car park, up through the narrow streets of Frigiliana was to me, with my hangover still not quite in abeyance, not its usual pleasant self. We passed the pretty courtyards bedecked with flowers and plants, and the squares with gaily coloured tables, chairs, and sun umbrellas, laid out, already serving drinks and meals, but instead of relishing in the beauty of these things, as I normally did, all I could think of was my head, which was still aching somewhat, and how much longer would it be before we got to Tony's house, and I could sit down in the shade for a while.

Suddenly my head exploded, or at least it felt like it did, for we were outside The 17th Century church of San Antonio de Padua, which is the main church in Frigiliana, and very close to Tony's house, and the bells had started to ring, as if to herald our arrival.

A couple of minutes later, we were at Tony's door, and being ushered in. This was definitely him, alive and well, there was no doubt about that, and if you needed further proof, I think the highly polished upright piano that greeted us as we went into the house, said all that was needed to be said on the subject. Village houses in Frigiliana are not exactly large, they are usually quite narrow, with just a couple of rooms on each floor, and Tony's was no exception. This was the reason, he later told us, that he finally had to sell his beloved Steinway Grand Piano, and buy the much smaller upright, there simply wasn't room for the Steinway.

He couldn't stop laughing when I told him that I had thought he had thrown himself off his terrace at the bar, 'but what about the note you left?' I asked, to which he explained that it was just part of his wicked sense of humour. I suppose it was nice to hear that he still had a sense of humour, after spending all those years in Nerja, building up a business, only to be stopped and almost ruined by a vindictive neighbour. But here he was, as large as life, living in this beautiful village, and dedicating all of his time now, to writing. When I say all of his time, I suppose I should say the majority of his time, because he still seems to find time to go out and eat, drink, and socialise, plus of course, he does play his wonderful new piano, and without any complaints from neighbours.

After a quick tour of his house, which included the roof terrace, which has wonderful views of the surrounding countryside and mountains, he grinned, as he showed us something else up there. It was his old neon sign from the bar, proclaiming "Sharp's Piano Bar". He has it mounted on a wall on the terrace, and can switch it on when he wants, but, he said that he doesn't do this very often in case anyone thinks that he is running an illegal bar from his home. A nice little bit of nostalgia to keep though.

A little while later, he took us across the street to a little bar/restaurant, where we had a delicious meal, consisting of several raciones of different dishes, including fish, salad, vegetables, and lamb cutlets, plus several drinks each, and the whole meal came to under 25 Euros. And people say Spain is becoming expensive? Not if you know where to go it isn't!

Back at Tony's after the meal, he seemed to have a never-ending supply of drink, which he kept insisting that we, especially me, tried. I am not exactly into spirits at the best of times, apart from Brandy, that is, so I am afraid I had to turn down Tony's hospitality when all these various spirits, some of which I had never even heard of, started to make their appearance. What I did enjoy immensely, was Tony, entertaining us with some wonderful tunes on his piano.

One thing however, did worry me somewhat, and that was the fact that Tony told us that he was now suffering from gout, which as everyone knows, is a terribly painful ailment, which if left untreated, can permanently damage joints and cause severe disability. With Frigiliana being such a hilly place, and his house having so many stairs, I wouldn't say that it was the perfect location for anyone suffering from gout, even though he says that he is now taking a daily dose of tablets to keep it under control. But I would imagine that Tony had taken this into account before deciding to move up there, as the gout had started whilst he was still down in Nerja. Knowing Tony as I do however, I think that he will overcome any future obstacles, get on with his life, and live it to its fullest, as he always has done.

Not long before we left, I noticed a photo of Tony's cat, Tabsy, on the wall, and I asked him if he was going to get another one. He seemed almost horrified at this idea, almost as if I had suggested someone getting a replacement parent after one had died. 'In fact' he said, 'next week, I am going to see a spiritualist in Malaga, who believes she can contact Tabsy'.

I do not particularly believe in spiritualists, but I do believe in the power of the spirit, especially if it comes in alcoholic form. So was it a real spirit, or just that magical power that caused me to see the keys of his piano move, silently, of their own accord, just before we left? If it really was Tabsy, why would his ghost want to play the piano, wouldn't it have been better employed, hanging around the fridge, meowing for a bowl of milk, or some delicious gambas perhaps?

As I drove back to Nerja that afternoon, I smiled to myself as I thought of all the things I had thought about what had possibly happened to Tony. I also thought of all the good times I had spent in his bar in the past, and of the great afternoon my wife and I had just spent with him in Frigiliana.

I have of course, seen Tony several times since then, and apart from a relatively short stint in hospital, connected to his gout of course, he is doing absolutely fine, and still playing brilliant piano. And I am sure that he will be playing for a long time yet to come!

Sharp's Piano Bar in Calle Carabeo, is alas, no more. I walked past it just a few months after that first visit to Tony in Frigiliana, and saw that the developers had already pulled the whole building down. I looked through the metal grill at the piles of rubble which was all that remained of the actual bar, but at the far end, the terrace still remains, complete with two plastic chairs, facing the sea. One for Tony, and the other for Tabsy, perhaps? There is now a house built on the site of the old bar.

Chapter 12

As you will have no doubt worked out by now, this is not a typical travel guide, pointing out to you the opening times of museums, and what time the last bus leaves to take you to the airport. There are so many leaflets and pamphlets available from local tourist offices, holiday villa rental companies, and even estate agents and free local newspapers, which dish out all those facts, that I honestly cannot see the point of including such mundane pieces of information in a book such as this, which is really a reflection of my personal travels and experiences in this region.

When I first started to write this book, I posed a question to myself, asking myself why I loved Nerja so much, and what makes it so special to so many people. Looking back at it now, I suppose this was more a hypothetical question than anything else. I think that most people who come to Nerja, think of it as their special place, I know I do, and I have heard this said so many times by different people.

Nerja is a special place, for various reasons to different people, and because we all love it so much, we feel that we have to tell other people about it, but that is where problems just might begin. Because the more people I tell about it, the less likely it is to stay the way I remember it and love it. I have been going back and forth to Nerja since 1996, not exactly a long time I admit, but in that short period I have got to know so many people and so many places, both in Nerja and in the other nearby towns and villages that I have mentioned, that I feel that I am a part of them all.

What I have tried to show in this book, are my personal views of this area, in the hope that you, the reader, will also enjoy the experiences that I have enjoyed, and hopefully find new experiences of your own. You won't find Tony's bar any more, but I am sure that you will find other bars and restaurants and interesting characters, just as I did.

This book is dedicated to the pleasure seekers of this world, please enjoy it.

24247403R00063

Printed in Poland
by Amazon Fulfillment
Poland Sp. z o.o., Wrocław